THE REFORMERS AND PURITANS AS SPIRITUAL MENTORS

"Hope is kindled"

THE REFORMERS AND PURITANS AS *SPIRITUAL MENTORS*

Michael A.G. Haykin

joshua
press

p r e s s
www.joshuapress.com

Published by
Joshua Press Inc., Kitchener, Ontario, Canada
Distributed by
Sola Scriptura Ministries International
www.sola-scriptura.ca

First published 2012

Cover and book design by Janice Van Eck

*The publication of this book was made possible by the generous support of
The Ross-Shire Foundation*

A note on the primary sources
The spelling of the English cited in the sources in the text has generally been
modernized, as has the use of capitals.

Library and Archives Canada Cataloguing in Publication

Haykin, Michael A. G.
    The reformers and Puritans as spiritual mentors :
hope is kindled / Michael A.G. Haykin.

(The Christian mentor ; v.2)
Includes bibliographical references and index.
Issued also in electronic format.

ISBN 978-1-894400-39-8

    1. Reformation—England—Biography. 2. Reformers—England—Biography.
3. Puritans—England—Biography. 4. Church history—Modern period, 1500–.
I. Title. II. Series: Christian mentor (Kitchener, Ont.) ; v.2.

BR378.H39 2012   270.6092'2   C2011-906136-8

For six dear brothers who have been
mentors to me in my Christian life

Bruce Woods
Ted Barton
Jacques Alexanian
Bill Payne
Bob Holmes
David Puckett

Contents

1

The Reformers and Puritans in their historical context

An introductory word

> May the inward light of thy Spirit lead us to the light of thy word.—JOHN CALVIN[1]

There is an engraving found in various Protestant contexts—a common British nineteenth-century rendition usually entitled it "The Candle of Reformation is Lighted"—that depicts all of the leading Reformers—including some voices for reform from the Middle Ages, men such as John Wycliffe (*c*.1330–1384) and Jan Hus (*c*.1369–1415)— gathered around a table upon which a single, shining candle burns. The engraving portrays the main achievement of the Reformers: the

---

1 Prayer at the close of Calvin's lecture on Zechariah 3:9–4:6 in *Commentaries on the Twelve Minor Prophets*, trans. John Owen (Reprint, Grand Rapids: William B. Eerdmans Publ. Co., 1950), 5:112.

unveiling of the light of the gospel in Europe after a long eclipse and period of spiritual darkness. By unveiling that light the Reformers were once more placing God as he has revealed himself in Christ at the centre of the church's life and thought.[2]

THE REFORMATION AND THE WORD OF GOD

The two areas in which this theocentric agenda of the Reformers had its greatest impact were, first, the doctrine of salvation as the doctrine of justification by faith alone was rediscovered, and, second, the church's worship. It is usually only the first area that is recalled when the Reformation is mentioned. But there was a clear and urgent desire on the part of the Reformers to also effect definite reform in the worship of the mediæval Roman Catholic church. As they measured that worship against Scripture they found that it was riddled with superstitious rites and taken up with undue emphasis on the proper performance of certain external actions, all of which tended to obscure the Word of God. Martin Luther (1483–1546), the pioneer of the German Reformation, thus analyzed the situation of his day:

> Three great abuses have befallen the service of God. First, God's Word is not proclaimed; there is only reading and singing in the Churches. Second, because God's Word has been suppressed, many unchristian inventions and lies have sneaked into the service of reading, singing and preaching, and they are horrible to see. Third, such service of God is being undertaken as a good work by which one hopes to obtain God's grace and salvation. Thus faith has perished and [instead of believing the gospel] everyone wishes to endow churches or to become a priest, monk or nun.[3]

From Luther's perspective, the failure of the mediæval church lay in its refusal to give the Word of God free course. The solution obviously

---

2   Carl R. Trueman, *Reformation: Yesterday, Today & Tomorrow* (Bridgend: Bryntirion Press/Dundas: Joshua Press, 2000), 15.

3   Cited Wilhelm Pauck, "The Ministry in the Time of the Continental Reformation" in H. Richard Niebuhr and Daniel D. Williams, eds., *The Ministry in Historical Perspectives* (New York: Harper & Brothers, 1956), 111.

lay in the powerful proclamation of the Word of God. Luther himself knew the impact of that Word by personal experience. As he commented in the early days of the Reformation as to why the Reformation was happening:

> I simply taught, preached, and wrote God's Word; otherwise I did nothing. And while I slept, or drank Wittenberg beer with my friends..., the Word so greatly weakened the papacy that no prince or emperor ever inflicted such losses upon it. I did nothing; the Word did everything.[4]

The English Reformer, Hugh Latimer (c.1485–1555), the Bishop of Worcester, could similarly declare: "*Scala coeli* [the ladder of heaven] is a preaching matter...and not a massing matter. God's instrument of salvation is preaching."[5] It is noteworthy that the leading term used by these Reformers to describe the minister was "preacher." The term "pastor" (the more common term today), though employed by the Reformers, would only come into regular use in Protestant, Reformed and Evangelical circles in the eighteenth century.[6]

Another example of this emphasis of the Reformers can be found in the approach of John Calvin (1509–1564) to the Scriptures and their purpose. When Calvin speaks about the nature of Scripture, his position is unambiguous. The Scriptures, he says, are "the pure Word of God," "free from every stain or defect," "the certain and unerring rule."[7] For Calvin the Bible is an inerrant and infallible book.[8] Unlike all other texts, these alone are a sure and certain guide for the believer's life and thinking. Moreover, Calvin assumed that Scripture, rightly interpreted,

---

4 "The Second Invocavit Sermon" in Ronald J. Sider, ed., *Karlstadt's Battle with Luther: Documents in a Liberal-Radical Debate* (Philadelphia: Fortress Press, 1978), 24.

5 Cited John B. Webster, "Ministry and Priesthood" in Stephen Sykes and John Booty, eds., *The Study of Anglicanism* (London: SPCK/Philadelphia: Fortress Press, 1988), 287.

6 Pauck, "Ministry in the Time of the Continental Reformation," 116.

7 Cited John H. Gerstner, "The View of the Bible Held by the Church: Calvin and the Westminster Divines" in Norman L. Geisler, ed., *Inerrancy* (Grand Rapids: Zondervan Publishing House, 1980), 391.

8 Cited Gerstner, "Calvin and the Westminster Divines," 391.

will not be found to make false assertions. This was the basic presupposition of all his exegesis and preaching.

Calvin was also convinced that in the Scriptures God speaks clearly. As he said: "the office of preaching is committed to pastors for no other purpose than that God alone may be heard there."[9] For Calvin, as for the other Reformers, hearing is *the* key sense of the Christian man and woman. Genuine "faith," he once said, "cannot flow from a naked experience of things, but must have its origin in the Word of God."[10] Mediæval Roman Catholicism had majored on symbols and images as the means for cultivating Christian living and thinking. Most of the men and women in the Middle Ages were illiterate and dependent upon a few sermons they heard, the pictures and symbols they saw in the stained glass of their churches and possibly the religious plays they watched for any Bible knowledge they had. The Reformation, coming as it did hard on the heels of the invention of the printing press, turned to "words," both spoken and written, as the primary vehicle for cultivating faith and spirituality.

PURITANISM—A SPIRITUALITY OF THE WORD

This Reformation of which we have been writing had come to England during the reign of Henry VIII (1491–1547), though it was not until the reign of his son Edward VI (r.1547–1553) and that of his daughter Elizabeth I (r.1559–1603) that it got a firm footing.[11] In fact, after Elizabeth I ascended the throne there was no doubt that England was firmly within the Protestant orbit. The question that arose, though, was to what extent the Elizabethan church would be reformed according to Scripture. It soon become clear that Elizabeth was content with a church that was "Calvinistic in theology, [but] Erastian in Church order and government [ie. the state was ascendant over the church in these areas], and largely mediaeval in liturgy."[12] In response to this

---

9 Cited Brian M. Abshire, "Calvin and Powerful Preaching" in *Chalcedon Report* 403, (February 1999): 8.

10 Cited J. Nigel Westhead, "Calvin and Experimental Knowledge of God" in *Adorning the Doctrine. Papers read at the 1995 Westminster Conference* (London: The Westminster Conference, 1995), 18.

11 For more discussion of this, see chapters 2 and 3.

12 Robert C. Walton, *The Gathered Community* (London: Carey Press, 1946), 59.

ecclesiastical "settledness," there arose the Puritan movement in the early 1560s, which sought to reform the Elizabethan church after the Scriptural model of the churches in Protestant Switzerland, especially those in Geneva and Zürich. For a hundred years they stove for a deeper reformation of the state church, until, finally, in 1662, via the Act of Uniformity, that church expelled them.

Now, the Puritans were sons and daughters of the Reformation, and thus not surprisingly "Puritanism was first and foremost a movement centred in Scripture,"[13] and like the Reformers, they prized preaching above all the other means of grace.[14] Nicholas Bownde (d.1613), a Suffolk Puritan minister, who published the first major Puritan exposition of Sunday as the Sabbath, *A True Doctrine of the Sabbath* (1595), could declare that preaching the Word of God is "the greatest part of God's service."[15] The Elizabethan Puritan Richard Sibbes (1577–1635) was just as enthusiastic about preaching. "It is a gift of all gifts," he wrote, "God esteems it so, Christ esteems it so, and so should we esteem it."[16] And in the association records of the Northern Baptist Association, which was composed of Baptist churches in the old counties of Northumberland, Cumberland, Westmoreland and Durham, we read the following answer to the question posed in 1701 as to whether "any Preaching disciple may Administer the Ordinance of the Lords Supper and Baptisme": "Those Persons that the Church approves of to Preach the Gospel we think it safe to Approve likewise for ye Administering other Ordinances Preaching being the greater work." In 1703, when a similar question was asked, it was stated that "those whom the Church Approves to preach the Gospel may also Administer

---

13 Richard Dale Land, "Doctrinal Controversies of English Particular Baptists (1644–1691) as Illustrated by the Career and Writings of Thomas Collier" (Unpublished D.Phil. thesis, Regent's Park College, Oxford University, 1979), 205.

14 As Irwony Morgan puts it: "the essential thing in understanding the Puritans is that they were preachers before they were anything else." Cited John H. Primus, *Holy Time: Moderate Puritanism and the Sabbath* (Macon: Mercer University Press, 1989), 170. For details of such a preaching ministry, see chapter 6, which deals with Richard Greenham.

15 Cited Primus, *Holy Time*, 174.

16 *The Fountain Opened* in *Works of Richard Sibbes*, ed. Alexander B. Grosart (1862–1864; reprint, Edinburgh: The Banner of Truth Trust, 2001), V, 509.

the Ordinances of Baptism and the Lords Supper Preaching being the main and principall [sic] Work of the Gospel."[17]

Given this focus on preaching, it is not surprising that at the heart of the Puritan movement was a deep-seated desire to cultivate a spirituality of the Word that would lead to a life that was regulated by Scripture first and foremost. Indeed, this Word-centred spirituality lies at the very core of English Puritanism. Whatever else the Puritans may have been—social, political and ecclesiastical Reformers—they were primarily men and women intensely passionate about piety and Christian experience.[18] By and large united in their Calvinism, the Puritans believed that every aspect of their spiritual lives came from the work of the Holy Spirit. They had, in fact, inherited from the continental Reformers of the sixteenth century, and from Calvin in particular, "a constant and even distinctive concern" with the person and work of the Holy Spirit.[19] Benjamin B. Warfield (1851–1921), the distinguished American Presbyterian theologian, can actually speak of Calvin as "preeminently the theologian of the Holy Spirit."[20] And of his Puritan heirs and their interest in the Spirit, Warfield has this to say:

The formulation of the doctrine of the work of the Spirit waited for the Reformation and for Calvin, and...the further working out of the details of this doctrine and its enrichment by the profound study of Christian minds and meditation of Christian

---

17 S.L. Copson, *Association Life of the Particular Baptists of Northern England 1699–1732* (London: Baptist Historical Society, 1991), 89, 95.

18 Irvonwy Morgan, *Puritan Spirituality* (London: Epworth Press, 1973), 53–65, esp. 60; Dewey D. Wallace, Jr., *The Spirituality of the Later English Puritans. An Anthology* (Macon: Mercer University Press, 1987), xi–xiv; J.I. Packer, *A Quest for Godliness: The Puritan Vision of the Christian Life* (Wheaton: Crossway Books, 1990), 37–38.

19 Richard B. Gaffin, "The Holy Spirit," *The Westminster Theological Journal*, 43 (1980): 61. See also the detailed discussion by Garth B. Wilson, "Doctrine of the Holy Spirit in the Reformed Tradition: A Critical Overview" in George Vandervelde, ed., *The Holy Spirit: Renewing and Empowering Presence* (Winfield: Wood Lake Books, 1989), 57–62.

20 "Calvin's Doctrine of the Knowledge of God" in Samuel G. Craig, ed., *Calvin and Augustine* (Reprint, Phillipsburg: Presbyterian and Reformed Publishing Co., 1980) 107. See also "John Calvin: The Man and His Work" and "John Calvin the Theologian" in Craig, ed., *Calvin and Augustine*, 21, 487.

hearts has come down from Calvin only to the Puritans...it is only the truth to say that Puritan thought was almost entirely occupied with loving study of the work of the Holy Spirit, and found its highest expression in dogmatico-practical expositions of the several aspects of it...[21]

A USABLE PAST

The goal of reforming the Church of England eluded the grasp of the Puritans. If their movement be weighed against the achievement of this goal, it must be deemed a failure. But, as men and women imbued with a passion for the Word and its central personage, the Triune God, they are a model for all Christians with regard to the thoughts and affections—the piety—that ought to govern Christian action.

This idea of models and mentors is central to the contents of this book, the first in a series of studies (there are three currently planned) seeking to help present-day Christians lay hold of a "usable past." This latter term has become central to an ongoing discussion among historians about the relevance of the past. By employing it, I am signifying my commitment to the concept that the past does indeed have significance for the present and that the historian has a duty to share his historical studies with a public wider than the academic guild of historians and to help non-specialists see the way the light of the past can help illumine the present.[22] In this collection of essays and lectures—written for a variety of settings and over the period of the last fifteen or so years[23]—I am really seeking to follow a biblical principle that should undergird the Christian study of church history. That principle lies behind the admonition of Hebrews 13:7: "remember your leaders,

21 Benjamin B. Warfield, "Introductory Note" to Abraham Kuyper, *The Work of the Holy Spirit*, trans. Henri de Vries, 1900 ed. (Reprint, Grand Rapids: William B. Eerdmans Publ. Co., 1956), xxxv, xxviii.

22 See, for example, William Bouwsma, *A Usable Past: Essays in European Cultural History* (Berkeley/Los Angeles: University of California Press, 1990), 1ff, and K.S. Brown and Yannis Hamilakis, "The Cupboard of the Yesterdays? Critical Perspectives on the Usable Past," in Brown and Hamilakis, eds., *The Usable Past: Greek Metahistories* (Lanham: Lexington Books, 2003), 1ff.

23 I have sought to acknowledge in each case where the essay/lecture began its individual existence before being included in this collection.

who spoke the Word of God to you. Pondering carefully the outcome (*anatheōrountes tēn ekbasin*) of their way of life, imitate their faith."

How is the Christian community to view preachers and teachers of the past according to Hebrews 13:7? First, from the vantage-point of the preacher-author of Hebrews, present-day believers are to "continue to remember" such teachers or preachers. The use of the present imperative stresses a continual or ongoing remembrance.[24] And what is the nature of this remembrance? It is summed up first of all in the participle *anatheōrountes*. This word has the basic idea of looking at something again and again, examining it and observing it carefully.[25] One commentator defines the word thus: "to closely view with attention, to scrutinize closely."[26] Now, how is the participle being used here? Is it imperatival, thus indicating a command in addition to remember?[27] Or is it the means by which we remember?[28] Either way, it is a strong directive to spend time reflecting on the lives of past leaders in the church. And what especially is to be scrutinized? It is their "way of life," that is, the "sum total" or "achievement" of their day-to-day behaviour.[29] In fact, this is nothing less than an admonition to believers to be familiar with the history of Christian leaders. And

---

24 William L. Lane, *Hebrews 9–13* (Word Biblical Commentary, vol.47$_B$; Dallas: Word Books, 1991), 522, note a.

25 *A Greek-English Lexicon of the New Testament and other Early Christian Literature*, 3rd ed., ed. Walter Bauer, Frederick William Danker, W.F. Arndt and F.W. Gingrich (Chicago/London: University of Chicago Press, 2000), s.v [henceforth cited as BDAG[3]]. See also Lane, *Hebrews 9–13*, 522, note c.

26 Wayne Barber, Spiros Zodhiates, *et al.*, *Woodland Park Baptist Church: Constitution and Bylaws* (Chattanooga: Woodland Park Baptist Church, 2003), "Appendix I: On Hebrews 13:7", 22 (available at: http://www.woodlandpark.org/downloads/wpbcConstitution.pdf; accessed March 20, 2010).

27 Thus George J. Zemek, "The Modeling of Ministers" in Richard L. Mayhue and Robert L. Thomas, eds., *The Master's Perspective on Pastoral Ministry* (Grand Rapids: Kregel, 2002), 268, n.61.

28 Luke Timothy Johnson, *Hebrews. A Commentary* (Louisville: Westminster John Knox Press, 2006), 346: "'remembering' through 'gazing.'"

29 Philip Edgcumbe Hughes, *A Commentary on the Epistle to the Hebrews* (Grand Rapids: William B. Eerdmans Publ. Co., 1977), 569. On the interpretation of *ekbasis*, see especially BDAG[3], s.v.; Hughes, *Hebrews*, 569, n.18; Lane, *Hebrews 9–13*, 522, note d. Compare the desire of the writer in Hebrews 13:18.

why? So that they might imitate the faith-informed lives of these indi-viduals. The Christian past is indeed a "usable past" for it contains mentors for the living of the Christian life.

Here then is a key reason for the study of church history. The Chris-tian past is indeed a "usable past" for it contains mentors for the living of the Christian life. It is vital to note that this is not hagiography, for undergirding the command to imitate past leaders and mentors is the object of those individuals' faith: "Jesus Christ, the same yesterday and today and forever" (Hebrews 13:8). It is because Christ Jesus was at the centre of their preaching and living that their lives can be imitated today, for the Christ never changes. Their Lord is our Lord. Hebrews 13:8 is not an ontological statement, as some have taken it, but an assertion that the faith of the preachers can be imitated since the one they proclaimed, and in whom they had put their faith, namely, Jesus Christ, was ever the same.[30]

"HOPE IS KINDLED"

In this present collection of essays we look first, therefore, at the lives of William Tyndale, Thomas Cranmer and John Calvin, among the Reformers, seeking to see how their display of the light of the gospel in their far-off day might provide us with models of Christian convic-tion and living for our own. They were born in a time of spiritual darkness—I am of the old school of Protestant historiography that believes the Reformation to have been very necessary—and, in many ways, our day in the West is a day of deepening twilight in both church and culture. As such, these models of what reformation involves for both of these realms is helpful: a deep commitment to God's Word as the vehicle of Reformation (Tyndale), a willingness to die for the gospel (Cranmer) and a rock-solid commitment to the Patristic vision of the triune God (Calvin). An essay on two Reformation confessions is also included as a reminder that it is not only people from our past that are helpful guides but also texts and that at the heart of the Reformation is a confessional Christianity, which is so deeply needed today.

---

30 David A. de Silva, *Perseverance in Gratitude: A Socio-Rhetorical Commentary on the Epistle "to the Hebrews"* (Grand Rapids: William B. Eerdmans Publ. Co., 2000), 494–495; Lane, *Hebrews 9–13*, 528.

The Puritan figures studied in this collection are the early Puritan leader Richard Greenham, who shows us the importance of soul care. Then we look at four Stuart Puritans: Oliver Cromwell, a man of action who had as rich a grasp of Scripture as any preacher of his time—a great reminder that public and political life need not be a godless life; John Owen, whose pastoral pneumatology is vital for us today; Richard Baxter and his wife Margaret, who model for us biblical marriage; and finally, John Bunyan, whose mini-treatise on prayer in the Spirit is an important reflection on a central way that we draw near to God. I have also included a recent study of the King James Bible (KJB), prepared for the quatercentenary of its publication, since the Puritans, like the Reformers, were Word-saturated men and women.

There is a common thread uniting the men, women and texts studied in these essays and lectures: they are a reminder that God is ever at work among his people. In the movie version of the twentieth-century epic *The Lord of the Rings*, there is a powerful, deeply emotive scene where the signal beacons atop the hills and mountains between Gondor and Rohan are lit, one by one, over the many miles separating the two realms, renewing the alliance between these two ancient peoples and foreshadowing the ultimate triumph of light over darkness.[31] In J.R.R. Tolkien's original text, the lighting of these beacons prompts Gandalf to thus comment on their meaning: "War is kindled."[32] But Peter Jackson, in his cinematic rendition of Tolkien's epic, has Gandalf respond quite differently. When the beacons are lit, the wizard remarks, "Hope is kindled."[33] When God lit the candle of the Reformation, which was still burning brightly in the days of the Puritans, it was not simply for that day. It was for us as well, kindling hope in the God who acted so powerfully on their behalf that he will act so for us and for his glory.

---

31 M.I. Kim, "Hope in Peter Jackson's *The Lord of the Rings*" (http://archive.thejujube. com/Themes/hopeinlotr.html; accessed April 7, 2011).

32 J.R.R. Tolkien, *The Return of the King*, vol. 3 of *The Lord of the Rings*, 2nd ed. (London/Sydney: Unwin Hyman, 1966), 19.

33 See the insightful analysis of Kim, "Hope in Peter Jackson's *The Lord of the Rings*." The words of Jackson's Gandalf were recently drawn to my attention by my good friend, the Rev. Joe Boot of Toronto, Ontario.

2

"The father of the English Bible"

William Tyndale

To scatter Roman darkness by this light
The loss of land and life I'll reckon slight.
—WILLIAM TYNDALE[1]

In 1994, the British Library paid the equivalent of well over $2,000,000 for a book which Dr. Brian Lang, the chief executive of the Library at the time, described as "certainly the most important acquisition in our 240-year history." The book? A copy of the New Testament. Of course, it was not just any copy. In fact, there are only two other New Testaments like this one in existence. One of those, that in the library of St. Paul's Cathedral, London, is lacking seventy-one of its pages. The

---

1   This quote is one translation of the couplet under the Tyndale portrait that hangs in the dining-hall of Hertford College, Oxford. See the front cover of David Daniell, *William Tyndale. A Biography* (New Haven/London: Yale University Press, 1994) for this portrait.

third one, very recently discovered in the Landesbibliothek in Stuttgart, Germany, is the only one of the three extant with a title-page.[2] The New Testament that the British Library purchased was lodged for many years in the library of the oldest Baptist seminary in the world, Bristol Baptist College, Bristol, England. It was printed in the German town of Worms (pronounced "warms") on the press of Peter Schöffer the younger, a competent die-cutter and printer, in 1526, and is known as the Tyndale New Testament. The first printed New Testament to be translated into English out of the original Greek, it is indeed an invaluable book. The 700 or so pages of text of this New Testament are in a black-letter or Gothic font and printed in a compact octavo format, clearly designed to be carried with ease. There are no verse divisions, which did not come into vogue until the Geneva New Testament of 1557, but only simple chapter breaks. It is devoid of prologue and marginal notes, both of which would be found in later editions of the Tyndale New Testament and other later Tudor Bibles. Its translator, after whom it is named, was William Tyndale (c.1494–1536). Of his overall significance in the history of the church, the article on him in the famous eleventh edition of the *Encyclopædia Britannica* rightly states that he was "one of the greatest forces of the English Reformation," a man whose writings "helped to shape the thought of the Puritan party in England."[3]

EARLY YEARS AND HISTORICAL CONTEXT

Though we know the general area in which Tyndale was born—the county of Gloucestershire next to Wales—we have no idea of the exact town or village in which he first saw the light of day. David Daniell, his most recent biographer suggests that the "most likely region of his origin is within a few miles of Dursley, between Bristol and Gloucester."[4] Nor do we know the exact date of his birth—the usually cited date of

---

2   Paul D. Wegner, *The Journey from Texts to Translations: The Origins and Development of the Bible* (Grand Rapids: Baker, 1999), 291; David Daniell, "Introduction" to William Tyndale, trans., *The New Testament. A Facsimile of the 1526 Edition* (London/ Peabody: The British Library/Hendrickson, 2008), ix–x.

3   *The Encyclopædia Britannica*, 11th ed. (New York: Encyclopædia Britannica, Inc., 1911), 27:499.

4   Daniell, *William Tyndale*, 9.

1494 is most probable, though not altogether certain. Nor is the identity of his parents known, although it is evident that he came from a
family that "included reasonably wealthy merchants and landowners."[5]
Indeed, the details of his early life are also shrouded in obscurity. Our
first solid evidence of him is in the first decade of the sixteenth century
when he was a student at Oxford University—he obtained his B.A.
there in 1512—and then later studying at Cambridge.[6]

It was at Cambridge that he would have definitely encountered the
works of the Dutch Renaissance scholar Desiderius Erasmus (c.1466–
1536), the foremost scholar of his day in western Europe and a satirical
critic of the morals and lifestyle of the clergy and leadership of the
Roman Catholic Church. Early sixteenth-century Europe was under-
going a series of massive transformations during the lifetime of
Tyndale—social, political, religious and intellectual—and Erasmus
proved to be a prime catalyst in the process of change. In the hope of
recovering the life and experience of the early church, Erasmus had
printed a copy of the New Testament in Greek in 1516 (revised editions
appeared in 1519, 1522, 1527 and 1535).[7] Prior to this point in time,
the New Testament was only generally available in western Europe
in a Latin translation dating from the end of the fourth century, a
translation that by the late Middle Ages definitely obscured a number
of key areas of Christian doctrine. Erasmus openly expressed the
desire that his Greek New Testament would be read by many of the
working-class in Europe and that it would reveal the vast difference
between the simplicity of New Testament Christianity and the degen-
erate state in which the Roman Church found itself at the beginning
of the sixteenth century.

Erasmus, it should be noted, was content to critique the morals of
the Roman Church. Its doctrine, in many areas just as aberrant as its
morals, he did not really view as a problem. But those who read the

---

5   Daniell, *William Tyndale*, 10–11.
6   Daniell, *William Tyndale*, 9.
7   The first printed Greek New Testament appears to have been the Complutensian
Polyglot version of the New Testament, which was printed 1514. This is clearly indi-
cated at the back of the book. Proof of this I saw in a copy owned by David Lachmann
of Philadelphia, Pennsylvania.

Greek New Testament, men like Martin Luther as well as Tyndale himself, came to the realization that nothing was going to change with regard to the morals of Rome until there was a return to New Testament doctrine. This is one of the most decisive differences between the Reformers and various critics of the morality of the Roman Church like Erasmus. The former found the ground of the Roman Church's corruption in her doctrinal errors, while the latter were content to criticize the moral failings of the Church and recommend a return to the simplicity of life in the New Testament church. For critics like Erasmus doctrine was not an issue. J.I. Packer and O.R. Johnston, in the introduction to their translation of Luther's *The Bondage of the Will*, compare Erasmus' programme of church renewal to a person going on a diet: the problem was simply the removal of some surplus pounds or excess fat. To the Reformers, including Tyndale, however, Christianity was a matter of doctrine first and foremost, because true religion was first and foremost a matter of faith and faith is inextricable from truth and doctrine.[8]

TO TRANSLATE THE SCRIPTURES INTO ENGLISH

It was probably during his time at Cambridge around 1520 that Tyndale came to evangelical convictions. In 1521 he left Cambridge University to become chaplain and private tutor in the home of Sir John Walsh at Little Sodbury Manor, a Cotswold house twelve or so miles south of Stinchcombe, Gloucestershire. It was while in Walsh's employ that Tyndale came to another firm conviction. He came to see that the printing of the New Testament in Greek was merely the first step in reforming the church. Since it was in Greek, it still remained a closed book to all who were not scholars and who could not read that language. Tyndale therefore determined to translate God's Word into English.

In strong contrast to mediæval Roman Catholicism where piety was focused on the proper performance of certain external actions, the Reformers emphasized that at the heart of Christianity was faith, which presupposed an understanding of what was believed. Knowledge of the Scriptures was therefore essential to Christian spirituality. Thus, Tyndale later stated in his preface to the Pentateuch: "I...perceived

---

8   J.I. Packer and O.R. Johnston, "Introduction" to their trans. of Martin Luther, *The Bondage of the Will* (Westwood: Fleming H. Revell Co., 1957), 42–45.

William Tyndale
c.1494–1536

by experience, how that it was impossible to establish the lay people in any truth, except the scripture were plainly laid before their eyes in their mother tongue."[9]

Nothing better reveals Tyndale's determination to translate God's Word than the story of what took place one evening during his time in Sir John Walsh's household. Walsh was an extremely hospitable man, and it often transpired that there were guests for dinner. On this occasion, according to Richard Webb of Chipping Sodbury, who was a servant of the Reformer Hugh Latimer, a high-ranking cleric was present, and Tyndale was outlining the problems of the Church of Rome in the light of God's Word. The cleric responded by saying that he would rather have the Pope's laws than those of the Word of God. His response and general tone of his conversation revealed a profound ignorance of God's Word and its preciousness. Tyndale, amazed by the man's words and his disdain for the Scriptures, replied, "I defy the Pope and all his laws,…if God spare my life, ere many years I will cause a boy that driveth the plough shall know more of the scripture than thou dost."[10]

In England, however, it was illegal to translate the Scriptures into English, let alone for a ploughboy to read them in his own native tongue. A law actually forbidding such a translation had been passed in 1408 after John Wycliffe, the so-called "morning star of the Reformation," had translated the Old and New Testaments from Latin into Middle English in the hope of bringing about a reform of the church. To stifle the aims of Wycliffe and his followers, known as the Lollards, it had been made illegal to put the Scriptures into English, to have such a translation in one's possession, or even to read such a translation without express permission of a bishop. And one of the main reasons why the church would not permit this was that a number of key Roman Catholic doctrines—for instance, the idea that there are seven sacraments or that there is a place called purgatory—cannot be found anywhere in the New Testament.[11] But Tyndale was not to be deterred from the pursuit of what he was coming to regard as God's calling for his life.

---

9   David Daniell, ed., *Tyndale's Old Testament* (New Haven/London: Yale University Press, 1991), 4.

10   Daniell, *William Tyndale*, 79.

11   Daniell, *William Tyndale*, 100.

Initially Tyndale sought for a wealthy and powerful patron who would support him in his translation work. He approached the Bishop of London, Cuthbert Tunstall (1474–1559), reputedly a friend of Erasmus, for such patronage, but to no avail.[12] Soon Tyndale came to the conviction that he would need to go abroad to the Continent to undertake such a translation. So, in April, 1524, he sailed from England for the port of Hamburg, Germany, little knowing that he would never see his native land again.

THE TYNDALE NEW TESTAMENT

He spent a year or so in Wittenberg, where he met the great German Reformer Martin Luther. He could have stayed in Wittenberg and translated the Scriptures in relative security and with all of the scholarly aids that he needed. Instead he chose to go to Cologne, one of the three great trading-ports of north-east Europe. Possibly he wanted to distance himself from Luther with whom he had a few minor theological disagreements. They disagreed, for instance, about the nature of the Lord's Supper—Luther holding to the "real presence" of the body and blood of Christ in the elements after the prayer of consecration, while Tyndale stressed the Lord's Supper as a commemoration of the death of Christ. Thus Tyndale could state:

> "The Lord Jesus, the night that he was betrayed, took bread, and gave thanks, and brake it, and said, Take, eat; this is my body that shall be given for you: this do in remembrance of me. And likewise he took the cup, when supper was done, saying, This cup is the new testament in my blood; this do, as often as ye shall drink it, in the remembrance of me." Here ye see by these words, that it was ordained to keep the death of Christ in mind, and to testify that his body was given and his blood shed for us. And, Luke 22: "This is my body, that is given for you; this do in remembrance of me. And this cup is the new testament in my blood, which shall be shed for you." Lo, here ye see again that it was instituted to keep the death of Christ in mind; and to testify wherefore he died,

---

12 Erasmus had great praise for Tunstall. But, as Tyndale rightly noted, Erasmus' "tongue maketh of little gnats great elephants" (Daniell, ed., *Tyndale's Old Testament*, 4)!

even to save us from sin, death and hell, that we should seek none other means to be delivered with; for there is none other name for us to be saved by, but only by the name of Jesus. Acts 4....the cause of the institution was to be a memorial, to testify that Christ's body was given, and his blood shed for us.[13]

Yet, it should be noted that there was solid agreement between the two men on the essentials of the faith. For instance, listen to Tyndale on justification:

To believe that Christ died for us is to see our horrible damnation, and how we were appointed unto eternal pains, and to feel, and to be sure, that we are delivered therefrom through Christ: in that we have power to hate our sins and to love God's commandments. All such repent, and have their hearts loosed out of captivity and bondage of sin, and are therefore justified through faith in Christ.[14]

And this on faith:

Right faith is a thing wrought by the Holy Ghost in us, which changeth us, turneth us into a new nature, and begetteth us anew in God, and maketh us the sons of God, as thou readest in the first of John; and killeth the old Adam, and maketh us altogether new in the heart, mind, will, lust, and in all our affections and powers of the soul; the Holy Ghost ever accompanying her, and ruling the heart. ...Faith is, then, a lively and a steadfast trust in the favor of God, wherewith we commit ourselves altogether unto God; and that trust is so surely grounded, and sticketh so fast in our hearts, that a man would not once doubt of it, though he should die a thou-

---

13 A *Brief Declaration of the Sacraments in his Doctrinal Treatises and Introductions to Different Portions of the Holy Scriptures*, ed. Henry Walter (Cambridge: Cambridge University Press, 1848), 356, 365.

14 *The Obedience of a Christian Man* (1528), ed. Richard Lovett (London: Religious Tract Society, n.d.), 153. I am grateful to Robin Compston of Kennington, London, for the use of this book.

sand times therefor. And such trust, wrought by the Holy Ghost through faith, maketh a man glad, lusty, cheerful, and truehearted unto God and unto all creatures: whereof, willingly and without compulsion, he is glad and ready to do good to every man, to do service to every man, to suffer all things, that God may be loved and praised, which hath given him such grace; so that it is impossible to separate good works from faith, even as it is impossible to separate heat and burning from fire. [15]

Whatever the reason for Tyndale's departure from Wittenberg, in Cologne he finished his translation of the New Testament from the Greek. Accompanying it were marginal notes, many of which he took from Martin Luther's translation of the Scriptures into German—an indication of his use of Luther's German New Testament, which had appeared in 1522.[16] All that has survived, however, is a manuscript down to Matthew 22, since, just as he was about to print it, he was betrayed to Roman Catholic authorities.

Tyndale managed to escape with his translation and made his way to Worms. There, on the printing press of Peter Schöffer, 3,000 or 6,000 copies[17] of the first printed New Testament to be translated into English out of the original Greek were run off. The books were then smuggled back into England on boats, hidden in bales of cloth, and Tyndale's dream of giving the common person the Word of God started to become a reality. By early 1526 they were being sold openly in England. Response from church authorities, however, was not slow in coming. When word of Tyndale's translation reached the ears of Cuthbert Tunstall, the Bishop of London began to scour the boats coming into English harbours and ports for the precious books. Many of the New Testaments were seized or even bought, and Tunstall had them publicly burned in the heart of London.

---

15 "A Prologue upon the Epistle of St. Paul to the Romans" in *Doctrinal Treatises*, 493.

16 Heinz Bluhm, "Martin Luther and the English Bible: Tyndale and Coverdale" in Gerhard Dünnhaupt, ed., *The Martin Luther Quincentennial* (Detroit: Wayne State University Press, 1984), 112–125.

17 It is not clear how large the print-run was exactly. See Daniell, *William Tyndale*, 134.

Tunstall claimed that the Tyndale New Testament was "naughtily translated"[18] and was an atrociously poor translation. Proof of the latter was the fact that he had reputedly found 3,000 errors in it. Tyndale noted that if a "t" was not crossed or an "i" not dotted, men like Tunstall counted it an error. Ironically, the money that was paid for the copies eventually found its way back to Tyndale, who simply used it to finance another edition! In fact, while there were places that Tyndale's translation could be improved—and Tyndale was not too proud to learn from criticism and incorporate changes into his two subsequent editions of the New Testament (a major revised edition appeared in 1534; there was another revision in 1535)—overall his translation was a superb piece of work. What is also noteworthy is that when Tyndale sat down to his translation, he basically had no one to guide him, there was no library at his disposal, no friendly scholar to check and critique his work. He had no access to books on the principles of translation.[19] It should be noted, though, that he did have Luther's translation as a rough model to follow.

SOME TRANSLATION DETAILS

There is little doubt that Tyndale had a solid handle on the Greek language, its idioms, shades of meaning and idiosyncrasies. A good example of his knowledge of Greek is found in Philemon 7, which Tyndale rightly translates, "For by thee (brother) the saints' hearts are comforted." The King James Bible (KJB) translators render this verse as "the bowels of the saints are refreshed by thee, brother," taking the Greek word *splanchna* literally as "bowels." Tyndale has rightly recognized that it is a metaphor for "heart." Of course, he got some things wrong. In James 4:2, for example, he has "ye envy," when the Greek actually has "you kill" (cf. KJB: "ye kill"). But overall it is now recognized that Tyndale was a brilliant Greek scholar. In fact, he had remarkable linguistic skills, being the master of at least eight languages, including Greek.

---

18 Cited Henry Wansbrough, "Tyndale" in Richard Griffiths, ed., *The Bible in the Renaissance: Essays on Biblical Commentary and Translation in the Fifteenth and Sixteenth Centuries* (Aldershot/Burlington: Ashgate, 2001), 129, modernized.

19 Brian H. Edwards, *God's Outlaw* (Welwyn: Evangelical Press, 1976), 99.

Equally important was his impressive grasp of the words and rhythms of the spoken English of his day. He knew how to render the Scriptures into the English vernacular so that they spoke with force and power. In fact, as David Daniell notes, what still strikes a contemporary reader is how modern Tyndale's translation actually is.[20] For instance, in contrast to the KJB rendering of Romans 5:2—"we have access by faith"—Tyndale has the much more modern sounding "we have a way in through faith."[21] "It is a sure thing" (Philippians 3:1)[22] is far more contemporary an expression than "it is safe" (KJB). Or consider his punchy version of 2 Kings 4:28—he began to work on the Old Testament in early 1530s—"thou shouldest not bring me in a fool's paradise." The KJB version is quite sedate in comparison, "do not deceive me."[23] In Hebrews 12:16, instead of the KJB's "as Esau, who for one morsel sold his birthright," Tyndale has Esau selling his birthright "for one breakfast." In fact, many of his words and phrases became part of everyday English—words and phrases such as "peacemaker," "longsuffering," the "salt of the earth," "fight the good fight," "God forbid," "the spirit is willing," "there were shepherds abiding in the fields," and "this thy brother was dead, and is alive again: and was lost, and is found." So good in fact was Tyndale's translation of the New Testament that, when the KJB translators came to fashion a new translation at the start of the seventeenth century, they went back to Tyndale's work and used no less than ninety per cent of it,[24] which also speaks volumes for his grasp of Greek.

Comparison, for example, of Tyndale's rendition of 1 Corinthians 13 in his 1534 edition with the same passage in the KJB reveals the great indebtedness of the KJB translators to Tyndale.

---

20 *William Tyndale*, 135.

21 *Tyndale's New Testament*, 229. For this example and those that follow, I am indebted to David Daniell, *The Bible in English: Its History and Influence* (New Haven/London: Yale University Press, 2003), 137.

22 *Tyndale's New Testament*, 291.

23 Daniell, *Bible in English*, 137.

24 Daniell, *William Tyndale*, 1. Henry Wansbrough has a lower percentage: "for the portions of the Bible translated by Tyndale, between 70 per cent and 80 per cent of the King James Version is verbatim Tyndale's version" ("Tyndale" in Griffiths, ed., *Bible in the Renaissance*, 127–128).

1534 *Tyndale New Testament*

Though I spake with the tonges of men and angels, and yet had no love, I were even as soundinge brasse: or as a tynklynge Cymball. And though I coulde prophesy, and understode all secretes, and all knowledge; yee, yf I had all fayth so that I could move mountayns oute of ther places, and yet had no love, I were nothynge. And though I bestowed all my gooddes to fede the poore, and though I gave my body even that I burned, and yet had no love, it profeteth me nothinge.

Love suffreth longe, and is corteous. Love envieth not. Love doth not frowardly, swelleth not, dealeth not dishonestly, seketh not her awne, is not provoked to anger, thynketh not evyll, reioyseth not in iniquitie: but reioyseth in the trueth, suffreth all thynge, beleveth all thynges, hopeth all thynges, endureth in all thynges. Though that propehsyinge fayle, other tonges shall cease, or knowledge vanysshe awaye, yet love falleth never awaye.

For oure knowledge is unparfect, and oure prophesyinge is unperfet. But when that which is parfect is come, then that which is unparfet shall bedone awaye. When I was a chylde, I spake as a chylde, I understode as a childe, I ymagened as a chylde. But assone as I was a man, I put away childesshnes. Now we see in a glasse even in a darke speakynge: but then shall we se face to face. Now I knowe unparfectly: but then shall I knowe even as I knowen. Now abideth fayth, hope, and love, even these thre: but the chefe of these is love.

1611 *King James Bible*

Though I speake with the tongues of men & of Angels, and have not charitie, I am become as sounding brasse or a tinkling cymbal. And though I have the gift of prophesie, and understand all mysteries and all knowledge: and though I have all faith, so that I could remoove mountaines, and have no charitie, I am nothing. And though I bestowe all my goods to feede the poore, and though I give my body to bee burned, and have not charitie, it profiteth me nothing.

Charitie suffereth long, and is kinde: charitie envieth not: charitie vaunteth not it selfe, is not puffed up, Doeth not behave it selfe unseemly, seeketh not her owne, is not easily provoked, thinketh no evil, Reioyceth not in iniquitie, but reioyceth in the trueth: Beareth all things, beleeveth all things, hopeth all things, endureth all things. Charitie never faileth: but whether there be prophesies, they shall faile; whether there bee tongues, they shall cease; whether there bee knowledge, it shall vanish away.

For we know in part, and we prophesie in part. But when that which is perfect is come, then that which is in part, shalbe done away. When I was a childe, I spake as a childe, I understood as a childe, I thought as a childe: but when I became a man, I put away childish things. For now we see through a glasse, darkely: but then face to face: now I know in part, but then shall I know even as also I am knowen. And now abideth faith, hope, charitie, these three, but the greatest of these is charitie.

As one can readily see from the extract from Tyndale, spelling in his day was far from being uniform. For instance, "imperfect" is spelt three different ways in three lines: "unparfect," "unperfet," and "unparfect"! It is not the case that Tyndale was a poor speller or that the printer did such a poor job in printing!

Now, there are two major differences between Tyndale and the KJB. One is the rendition of verse 12 and the other is the translation of the Greek word *agape*. The KJB renders this "charity" whereas Tyndale had translated it by "love." The KJB rendering was actually a step in the wrong direction. Whatever the word "charity" had meant in earlier centuries, by the sixteenth and seventeenth centuries the word "charity" was a technical term in Roman Catholic circles for the bestowal of alms on the poor. Tyndale rightly recognized that the word failed to capture the breadth of the Greek term *agape* and that the best English rendition of the latter was "love."

CONTROVERSY WITH THOMAS MORE

In fact, Tyndale had a significant debate with Sir Thomas More (1478–1535) in which his translation of *agape* played a part. In 1528, the Bishop of London wrote to Sir Thomas More, requesting that he examine the works of certain "sons of iniquity" and explain "the crafty malignity of these impious heretics" to "simpleminded people." He sent More examples of the Lutheran writers and gave him permission to read such books in order to lead an attack against them. Tyndale was not mentioned in the letter, but his New Testament must have been among the books sent to More. Other tracts by Tyndale, published while More was working on his book, seem to have convinced him that Tyndale was the greatest danger among the Lutheran writers. In 1529, Sir Thomas More launched an attack against the Reformers, especially Luther and Tyndale, in a volume called *A Dialogue Concerning Heresies*.

More's charges against Tyndale were broad. While he took issue with specific words in Tyndale's translation ("congregation" instead of "church," "senior" instead of "priest," "repentance" instead of "penance," "love" instead of charity," for example), he was more concerned with condemning Tyndale as a fraud, a hypocrite, a devil, a man "puffed up with pride and envy." In 1530, More also took an active part in a church council that condemned Tyndale's works.

Tyndale answered More in July 1531 in *An Answer unto Sir Thomas More's Dialogue*.[25] In it Tyndale confirms More's worst fears by appealing to the Scriptures as the ultimate authority to evaluate not only church doctrine but also church practice, and by attacking the church hierarchy. Tyndale also accused More of having traded his earlier humanist convictions for wealth and power. More replied a year later in a long work, *The Confutation of Tyndale*, in which he repeats and intensifies his attacks, advocates the burning of Tyndale's books, prophesies that Tyndale will burn in hell for his sins and supported the burning of heretics such as Tyndale.

TRANSLATING THE OLD TESTAMENT

After completing the translation of the New Testament, Tyndale turned his attention to the Old. His translation of Genesis, which appeared in 1530, was the first English translation ever made from a Hebrew text. Only a tiny handful of Oxford and Cambridge scholars, if any at all, knew this language. In fact, most of the ordinary population would have been astonished to discover that Hebrew had anything to do with the Bible. For them, all of their religion was wrapped up in Latin.[26] Translations of a number of other books of the Old Testament followed: including the rest of the Pentateuch in 1530 and Jonah in 1531.

Where Tyndale learned Hebrew we have no idea. It is quite unlikely he learned it in England, since so little Hebrew was known there in the 1520s. Hebrew studies only began to take root in England during the reigns of Elizabeth I and James I. He had to have learned it, therefore, on the Continent, probably in Germany. David Daniell suggests that Tyndale may have studied Hebrew at Wittenberg when he was there in the mid-1520s.[27] As with the Greek New Testament, Tyndale displays a wonderful facility for rendering the Hebrew Scriptures—a linguistic world utterly unlike any other in Europe at that time—into English. And coinages that he made—like "Jehovah," "Passover,"

25 *An Answere unto Sir Thomas Mores Dialoge*, ed. Anne M. O'Donnell and Jared Wicks, vol. 3, *The Independent Works of William Tyndale* (Washington: Catholic University of America Press, 2000).
26 Daniell, *William Tyndale*, 287.
27 Daniell, *William Tyndale*, 291, 299.

"scapegoat," "shewbread," and "mercy seat"—have become a part of standard English.

Jonah, incidentally, was an important book for the Reformers. Luther, for instance, translated it separately in 1526. At its heart is the account of the preaching of repentance to a terribly sinful nation—the powerful message of repentance despite the weakness of the preacher. Just as God's Word had been preached to the Ninevites with the threat of judgement if repentance was not forthcoming, so God's Word had to be preached to the English. Thus, Tyndale can say: "if thou confess with a repenting heart and knowledge and surely believe that Jesus is Lord over all sin, thou art safe. ...And beware of the leaven that saith we have power in our free will...to deserve grace."[28]

TWO WORD-PICTURES FROM HIS FINAL DAYS

By the early 1530s, Tyndale was living in Antwerp, from whence the smuggling of the Scriptures across to England could be easily carried out. In 1535, he was hard at work on translating the books of Joshua to 2 Chronicles, as well as making some minor revisions to his 1534 New Testament. The translation had not yet progressed beyond the manuscript stage when he was arrested on May 21 of that year. Tyndale was betrayed into the hands of Roman Catholic authorities by a certain Henry Phillips, an appalling and perfidious individual who was probably acting under orders from John Stokesley (c.1475–1539), the Bishop of London at the time.[29] A royal proclamation issued before March 6, 1529, had condemned his translation of Genesis and Deuteronomy. Another of June 22, 1530, condemned his Bible. He was imprisoned in the infamous prison of Vilvorde, six miles north of Brussels. There he was put on trial for heresy—specifically for being a Lutheran—found guilty and condemned to be burned to death. Two word-pictures from the last year of his life reveal the character of the man.

The first comes from a letter that he wrote in the Vilvorde prison in the autumn of 1535. It was found during the last century and is the only surviving example of his handwriting. Writing to the governor of the prison, the Marquis of Bergen, Tyndale says:

---

28 "Prologue to the Prophet Jonas" in *Doctrinal Treatises*, 465, 466.
29 Daniell, *William Tyndale*, 367–368.

I believe, right worshipful, that you are not ignorant of what has been determined concerning me [by the Council of Brabant]. Wherefore I beg your Lordship, and that by the Lord Jesus, that if I am to remain here [in Vilvoorde] through the winter, you will request the commissary to have the kindness to send me, from the goods of mine which he has, a warmer cap; for I suffer greatly from cold in the head, and am afflicted by a perpetual catarrh, which is much increased in this cell; a warmer coat also, for this which I have is very thin; a piece of cloth too to patch my leggings. My overcoat is worn out; my shirts are also worn out. He has a woollen shirt, if he will be good enough to send it. I have also with him leggings of thicker cloth to put on above; he also has warmer night-caps. And I ask to be allowed to have a lamp in the evening; it is indeed wearisome sitting alone in the dark. But most of all, I beg and beseech your clemency to be urgent with the commissary, that he will kindly permit me to have the Hebrew Bible, Hebrew grammar, and Hebrew dictionary, that I may pass the time in that study. In return may you obtain what you most desire, so only that it be for the salvation of your soul. But if any other decision has been taken concerning me, to be carried out before winter, I will be patient, abiding the will of God, to the glory of the grace of my Lord Jesus Christ: whose Spirit, I pray, may ever direct your heart. Amen.[30]

To the end Tyndale was intent on the study and translation of God's Word—that precious book that Tyndale knew God the Holy Spirit would use to shed the light of God's salvation throughout benighted Europe. It is unlikely his petition was granted.

The other word-picture comes from the day of his death, traditionally October 6, 1536. The executioner, in an act of mercy to Tyndale, strangled him before he lit the wood piled around him. According to the martyrologist John Foxe, the last words that Tyndale was heard to utter were "Lord! open the King of England's eyes."

Up until this point the king, Henry VIII, had been firmly opposed to the free circulation of Tyndale's translation, despite his break with

---

30 Daniell, *William Tyndale*, 379.

Rome over his desire to get a divorce from his first wife, Catherine of Aragon.[31] Yet, within a year of Tyndale's death, his New Testament was being openly published in England, though not under his name. That Tyndale was not recognized as the translator would not have bothered him.

THREE LESSONS FROM THE LIFE OF TYNDALE

What lessons, then, can we learn from Tyndale's life and career? First, his willingness to undergo immense hardship to see the translation of God's Word into English speaks to us of the preciousness of God's Word. As the psalmist puts it in Psalm 19:10, speaking of the commandments of God: "More to be desired are they than gold, yea, than much fine gold." This also was Tyndale's view of God's Word. In his "Prologue" to his translation of Genesis, he wrote in 1530:

> the Scripture is a light, and sheweth us the true way, both what to do and what to hope for; and a defence from all error, and a comfort in adversity that we despair not, and feareth us in prosperity that we sin not.[32]

Second, Tyndale's experience shows that whenever God's Word is faithfully proclaimed—in his case, translated—it will arouse opposition. There is no faithful display of God's Word without opposition from the world.

Third, it is a certainty that God's Word will accomplish that for which it has been given. As the Apostle Paul had said during his imprisonment for the sake of the gospel: although he was in prison, "the word of God is not chained" (2 Timothy 2:9). Through the incorporation of Tyndale's translation into the King James Bible, Tyndale's work gave shape, substance and backbone to English-speaking Christianity down to the present century.[33] Enshrined in the King James Bible, his

---

31 On the influence of Anne Boleyn for good, see "The Royal Household of Henry VIII. Part One: A Changed Ann Boleyn," *The Sword and the Trowel*, No. 2 (1997): 12–14.

32 *Doctrinal Treatises*, 399.

33 Iain Murray, "William Tyndale" (Talk at the Free Reformed Church of Dundas, Ontario, October 24, 1994).

New Testament lived on for centuries after his death. As David Daniell has noted in what is the definitive biography of Tyndale, it was Tyndale that, by the grace of God, made the English people a "People of the Book."[34]

A few years before his death, Tyndale had written the following in the preface to his book *The Parable of the Wicked Mammon* (1528) regarding his translation of the New Testament:

> Some man will ask, peradventure, Why I take the labour to make this work, inasmuch as they will burn it, seeing they burnt the gospel? I answer, In burning the new Testament they did none other thing than what I looked for: no more shall they do, if they burn me also, if it be God's will it shall so be.
>
> Nevertheless, in translating the New Testament I did my duty...[35]

What a glorious duty, though, it was! The impact of Tyndale's doing his duty is well seen in an event that took place nearly thirty years after he wrote these words. One of his friends, John Rogers (1500–1555), who played the central role in the 1537 publication of "Matthew's Bible" that included much of Tyndale's translation work, was on trial for heresy. It was during the reign of Mary I (1516–1558), known to history as "bloody Mary" because of her brutal execution of nearly 300 Protestants in a misguided attempt to take the evangelical Church of England back to Rome.[36] Rogers' case was being heard by Stephen Gardiner (1483–1555), Mary I's Lord Chancellor. At one point, Gardiner told Rogers: "thou canst prove nothing by the Scripture, the Scripture is dead: it must have a lively [ie. living] expositor." "No," Rogers replied, "the Scripture is alive."[37] Undoubtedly Rogers is think-

---

34 *William Tyndale*, 3.

35 *Doctrinal Treatises*, ed. Walter, 43–44.

36 For an excellent, albeit popular, overview of Mary's reign of religious terror, see Andrew Atherstone, *The Martyrs of Mary Tudor* (Leominster: Day One Publications, 2005). For a recent revisionist perspective, see Eamon Duffy, *Fires of Faith: Catholic England under Mary Tudor* (New Haven/London: Yale University Press, 2009).

37 *The Acts and Monuments of John Foxe*, ed. Stephen Reed Cattley (London: R.B. Seeley & W. Burnside, 1838), VI, 596. On Rogers, see especially Tim Shenton, *John Rogers—sealed with blood* (Leominster: Day One Publications, 2007).

ing of Hebrews 4:12, but his conviction is also rooted in the fact that Tyndale's rendering of the Scriptures in "English plain style"[38] had played a key role, by God's grace, in the Scriptures becoming a vehicle of life-changing power among the English people.[39]

---

38 Daniell, *Bible in English*, 158.

39 See Daniell, *Bible in English*, 157–159, for his discussion of the legacy of Tyndale.

3

"A setter-forth of Christ's glory"

Remembering the life and martyrdom of Thomas Cranmer

I pray God to grant that I may endure to the end.

—THOMAS CRANMER[1]

As a Calvinistic Baptist I owe a significant debt to early Anglicanism. My seventeenth-century forebears learned much of their Reformed

---

1   The quotation in the chapter title comes from *An Homily of the Salvation of Mankind by Only Christ our Saviour from Sin and Death Everlasting* in T.H.L. Parker, ed., *English Reformers*, vol. 26, *The Library of Christian Classics* (Philadelphia: Westminster Press, 1966), 266. The bulk of this chapter originally appeared as "'A Setter-Forth of Christ's Glory': Remembering the Life and Martyrdom of Thomas Cranmer," *The Banner of Truth*, 525 (June 2007): 1–15. Used by permission.

theology from Reformed ministers in the Church of England, and it was in the heart of that body that they were nurtured on the spirituality of the Reformation. And in the earliest days of that state church, no figure exercised as great an influence as the "reluctant martyr" Thomas Cranmer (1489–1556), the first Reformed Archbishop of Canterbury.[2]

Kenneth Brownell has argued that Thomas Cranmer's influence on the English-speaking Protestant world has been greater than that of any other figure except his contemporary John Knox (c.1510–1572), and the eighteenth-century preachers George Whitefield (1714–1770), John Wesley (1703–1791) and Jonathan Edwards (1703–1758). "Few men," Brownell writes, "did more to shape English Protestant spirituality and to drive into the soul of a nation the fundamentals of Protestant Christianity."[3] Nevertheless, unlike these other figures, Cranmer is not at all an easy person to study or understand. Brownell's article bears witness to this: it is entitled "Thomas Cranmer: Compromiser or Strategist?" What kind of man was Cranmer really? Was he an astute politician who accommodated himself during the reign of Henry VIII, who made him Archbishop of Canterbury, until such time as he could promote church reform without obstruction? Or was he a man out of his depth during the reign of Henry VIII, a man simply trying to stay alive as best as he could?[4] The burden of this chapter, though, portrays him as one who eventually shared to the full the common agenda of the other Reformers in Western Europe at the time.[5]

---

2   For the term "reluctant martyr" as a description of Cranmer, see Diarmaid MacCulloch, *Thomas Cranmer: A Life* (London/New Haven: Yale University Press, 1996), 618. MacCulloch's book is now the standard life of Cranmer. For a pamphlet summary of his book, see Diarmaid MacCulloch, *Who was Thomas Cranmer?* (The St George's Cathedral Lecture, No. 11; Perth: St George's Cathedral, 2004).

3   Kenneth Brownell, "Thomas Cranmer: Compromiser or Strategist?" in *The Reformation of Worship. Papers read at the 1989 Westminster Conference* (London: The Westminster Conference, 1989), 1. See also the wide-ranging reflections of MacCulloch, *Thomas Cranmer*, 612–632.

4   See also G.S.R. Cox, "Thomas Cranmer" in *Approaches to Reformation of the Church* (London: The Puritan and Reformed Studies Conference, 1965), 42–43.

5   On this common perspective shared by the Reformers, see Scott H. Hendrix, "Rerooting the Faith: The Coherence and Significance of the Reformation", *The Princeton Seminary Bulletin*, n.s. 21, no.1 (2000): 63–80.

EARLY LIFE, 1489–1532

Cranmer was born on July 2, 1489, the son of Thomas and Agnes Cranmer, members of the lower gentry. His early schooling was not entirely satisfactory, but that did not prevent him from entering Jesus College, Cambridge, in 1503, at the age of 14. Here Cranmer was in his element. He was, as Brownell reminds us, "fundamentally an academic."[6] Or as Geoffrey W. Bromiley has put it: "To look at Cranmer is to see first the face of a scholar."[7] He became one of the most learned men of his age. His reading knowledge of foreign languages, both ancient and modern, included Latin, Greek and Hebrew, as well as French, Italian and German. He was thus able, for instance, to translate the Hebrew Old Testament into Latin for his own personal use. In 1510 or 1511, Cranmer was elected a Fellow of Jesus College after having taken his B.A. degree there. And around 1520 he became a priest.[8]

Evangelical Christianity came to Cambridge around the time that he became a priest. During the early 1520s the Protestant cause was centred around meetings at the White Horse Inn in Cambridge, led by such figures as Robert Barnes (1495–1540) and Thomas Bilney (c.1495–1531).[9] Scholars writing on the English Reformation in the past have tended to place Cranmer among this group. However, as Diarmaid MacCulloch has noted in his exhaustive study of Cranmer, this really amounts to a posthumous bestowal of membership. There is no concrete evidence to place Cranmer among this group of early Reformers.[10]

It was a conversation in 1529 with the important churchman, Stephen Gardiner, whom we met briefly at the close of the previous chapter, that changed Cranmer's entire life. One of the topics of discussion on this occasion was what was quaintly termed the "Privy Matter" of King Henry VIII, namely his attempt to divorce Catherine of Aragon (1485–1536), his first wife. Catherine, a Spanish princess,

---

6 Brownell, "Thomas Cranmer," 3.

7 Geoffrey W. Bromiley, "Thomas W. Cranmer" in B.A. Gerrish, ed., *Reformers in Profile* (Philadelphia: Fortress Press, 1967), 165.

8 Peter Newman Brooks, *Cranmer in Context: Documents from the English Reformation* (Minneapolis: Fortress Press, 1989), 2.

9 Christopher Catherwood, "Thomas Cranmer" in *Five Leading Reformers* (Tain: Christian Focus, 2000), 133.

10 MacCulloch, *Thomas Cranmer*, 24–33.

had initially been married to Henry's older brother, Arthur. But Arthur had died in 1502 of what was then called "consumption," which in his case was probably pneumonia. Henry was subsequently married to Catherine to maintain an alliance between England and Spain against France. After five unsuccessful pregnancies, Catherine gave Henry a daughter, the future Mary I. But Henry desperately wanted a son. He feared that if he died without a son, England would be plunged again into a fratricidal dynastic war, like the one of the previous century known as the Wars of the Roses. This war had lasted on and off for thirty years (1455–1485) and had only ended when his father, Henry VII (1457–1509) wrested the crown from Richard III (1452–1485) at the Battle of Bosworth (1485).

A special papal dispensation had been granted to allow Henry to marry his brother's widow, but now Henry felt that this marriage was under God's curse because he could not have a son. And the more Catherine miscarried—she had a number of miscarriages after Mary's birth[11]—the more Henry became convinced of the validity of his perspective. So began his quest for divorce in 1527.[12]

The pope, Clement VII (1478–1534), was unwilling to grant Henry's desire for a divorce. The reason was simple. In 1527, Clement had unwisely sided with the French against the Spanish and the Spanish ruler Charles V (1500–1558)—also the Holy Roman Emperor before whom Martin Luther stood at the Diet of Worms—had sent an army into Italy and sacked Rome, and Clement had been forced to barricade himself in one of his castles. Catherine of Aragon was Charles' aunt, and there was no way that the pope was going to anger Charles again by shaming his aunt in the face of the whole of Roman Catholic Europe. So the pope, and his papal legate in England, Cardinal Thomas Wolsey (c.1475–1530), stalled for time.

By 1529, Henry was losing patience. Now it happened that in a conversation between Cranmer and Gardiner, Cranmer had suggested that the case of Henry's divorce be put before the universities of

---

11 For details, see G.W. Bernard, *The King's Reformation: Henry VIII and the Remaking of the English Church* (New Haven/London: Yale University Press, 2005), 3–4.

12 On Henry's campaign for this divorce and his reasoning about it, see Bernard, *King's Reformation*, 9–26.

Western Europe for the academics to judge the merits of it. Henry heard of this proposal, loved it and ordered Cranmer to draw up a treatise defending the rightness of his position. Cranmer went to live in London, and there he drew up a document that supported Henry's right to divorce.

Cranmer was subsequently made a chaplain to the king as a result of this treatise and went from being an obscure scholar to being an up-and-coming player on the scene of national politics. In 1532, he was sent to Germany to represent Henry's case before Charles V. While Cranmer was on the Continent, word reached him of the death of the Archbishop of Canterbury, William Warham (c.1450–1532). Cranmer was summoned home by the king to succeed him.

HENRY'S ARCHBISHOP

Cranmer served Henry faithfully as his archbishop and was a strong supporter of royal supremacy throughout his life. "He believed," in the words of historian Jasper Ridley, "that his primary duty as a Christian was to strengthen the power of the King."[13] Disobedience to a royal command was only permissible if carrying out the command involved a violation of one of God's laws. His view of church government was thus thoroughly Erastian. This would cause him much heartache in his career.[14] He thus actively participated in Henry's divorce of Catherine, which led to the formal break of the Church of England from the Roman Catholic Church and the declaration of Henry as the supreme head of the Church in England—what is known as the Act of Supremacy—in 1534. Catherine's daughter Mary never forgot, nor forgave, Cranmer for his involvement in her mother's being divorced. Although Cranmer was not involved in the marriage of Henry to his second wife, Anne Boleyn (c.1501–1536)—whom Catherine of Aragon once described as "the scandal of Christendom"[15]—he did crown her queen in 1533.[16]

---

13 Jasper Ridley, *Thomas Cranmer* (Oxford: Clarendon Press, 1962), 12.

14 Brownell, "Thomas Cranmer," 6–7.

15 "Anne Boleyn" (http://www.englishhistory.net/tudor/monarchs/boleyn.html; accessed May 10, 2011).

16 Brooks, *Cranmer in Context*, 24, 33.

Only three years later Cranmer presided over a second royal divorce. Anne had given birth to the child who would become Elizabeth I (1533–1603), and had then borne a stillborn child, and Henry was still desperately seeking a son. Convinced that he had been wrong to marry Anne, he divorced her on trumped-up adultery charges and had her executed. It is noteworthy that Cranmer did seek to save Anne Boleyn from the executioner. Later Cranmer also presided over Henry's divorce of Anne of Cleves (1515–1557) in 1540 and his divorce of Catherine Howard (c.1520/24–1542) two years later.

The fall of Anne Boleyn and her subsequent execution for treason was a severe blow to Cranmer, for Anne was a keen supporter of the evangelical cause. That Cranmer was, by this time, an evangelical in his sympathies is seen from a letter he wrote on April 27, 1535, to Arthur Plantagenet (d.1542), Viscount Lisle, an uncle of Henry VIII. Cranmer told Lisle that "the very papacy and the see of Rome" is to be detested, since papal laws have "suppressed Christ"; they have set up the pope as "a god of this world"; and they have "brought the professors of Christ into such an ignorance of Christ."[17]

The fall of another key figure in the government, Thomas Cromwell (1485–1540), in 1540 provoked a further crisis for Cranmer, for Cromwell too had been a firm supporter of the cause of the Reformation. Cromwell's fall meant a triumph for the foes of Reformed truth, chiefly Stephen Gardiner, the Bishop of Winchester and Thomas Howard (1473–1554), the third Duke of Norfolk, "the most powerful and implacable conservative among the leading lay nobility."[18] Gardiner and Norfolk secured the passage of what is known as *The Six Articles* (1539), which, among other things, reinforced the traditional doctrine of transubstantiation, clerical celibacy and auricular confession. With this swing towards traditional Roman Catholicism,

---

17 *The Lisle Letters*, ed. Muriel St Clare Byrne and selected Bridget Boland (Harmondsworth: Penguin Books, 1985), 122. On Cranmer's early theology, see Bernard, *King's Reformation*, 506–512. A very helpful outline of Cranmer's theological development can be found in J.I. Packer, "Thomas Cranmer's Catholic Theology" in *Honouring the People of God*, vol. 4, *The Collected Shorter Writings of J.I. Packer* (Carlisle: Paternoster Press, 1999), 238–243.

18 Diarmaid MacCulloch, *Tudor Church Militant: Edward VI and the Protestant Reformation* (London: Allen Lane/Penguin Books, 1999), 7.

Cranmer the evangelical was in danger. Yet he survived. Why?

One clear reason is that King Henry genuinely liked him. In Christopher Catherwood's words: "Henry found in Cranmer a rare man: someone he could actually trust."[19] A second reason was that Henry was not a traditional Catholic in his views.[20] By 1543, he had all but rejected purgatory and could look back on a career of destroying shrines and images with pleasure that he had done God's will. He also refused to believe that confirmation, unction and ordination were sacraments.[21] And yet, it is important to note that he never accepted justification by faith alone. However, with the passage of *The Six Articles* in 1539, Henry required clerical celibacy of all ministers in England. Cranmer acquiesced by sending his wife away to the Continent. This leads to a third reason why Cranmer survived. Simply put, he compromised. His compromising can be clearly seen in the sending of his wife back to the Continent and in his approval of the execution of the Lutheran preacher Robert Barnes. There is evidence that Cranmer was an unwilling player in all of this, but that does not remove his guilt.[22]

The last years of Henry's reign—Henry died early in 1547—were indeed a see-saw battle between the traditionalists and evangelicals. But when Henry died in 1547, he left the evangelicals, especially in the person of Edward Seymour (1500–1552), Duke of Somerset, the uncle of his son, the future King Edward VI (1537–1553), in an unassailable position to take over the reigns of government.[23]

"TUDOR CHURCH MILITANT"[24]

When Edward was crowned king by Cranmer on February 20, 1547, he was reminded by the archbishop that God was also giving him a

---

19 "Thomas Cranmer," 148.

20 For further discussion of Henry's religious convictions, see Bernard, *King's Reformation*, 228–243. Though his ruthless suppression of the monasteries makes him look anything but Erasmian, Bernard argues that Erasmian humanism "makes best sense" of Henry's religious views.

21 MacCulloch, *Tudor Church Militant*, 4–5.

22 Brownell, "Thomas Cranmer," 11–12.

23 MacCulloch, *Tudor Church Militant*, 7.

24 This sub-title is from MacCulloch, *Tudor Church Militant*.

spiritual sword as well as a temporal sword with which to rule. He therefore urged him to remember that he was "God's vice-regent and Christ's vicar" within the realm of England. He was to ensure that "God [was] truly worshipped, and idolatry destroyed, the tyranny of the bishops of Rome banished…, and images removed. These acts be signs of a second Josiah, who reformed the church of God in his days."[25] There was now no hiding where Cranmer stood.

By the end of 1547, the evangelicals around Edward who were being led by Cranmer had, amongst other reforms, enshrined justification by faith alone in the church's official statements. Clerical marriage had been approved. Key continental Reformers had been invited to come to England to help in the Reformation there, men such as the Strasbourg Reformer Martin Bucer (1491–1551), who went to Cambridge, Peter Martyr (1500–1562)—an Anglicized form of Pietro Martire Vermigli—who went to Oxford and Jan Łaski (1499–1560), a Polish Reformer. In line with the aims of the Reformation throughout Europe, the worship of the church had been reformed. Cranmer's work in regard to the latter is probably best seen in *The Book of Common Prayer* of 1552, which was intended to be the "basis of reformed Protestant worship,"[26] and which, as Peter Toon has noted, is "a near perfect embodiment of the principle of justification by faith."[27]

CRANMER'S REFORMATION THEOLOGY

One gets a marvellous insight into the heart of Cranmer's Reformed thought by looking at two of his written prayers. First, consider one of his collects. In the context of Christian worship the Latin term *collecta*, from which we get the English word "collect," refers to the "collecting" together of the various prayers of the congregation into a single prayer.[28] Such prayers, whose origin lies in late antiquity, are

---

25 Cited Brooks, *Cranmer in Context*, 39–40.

26 Diarmaid MacCulloch, "The Myth of the English Reformation," *Journal of British Studies*, 30 (1991): 7–9.

27 "Remembering Thomas Cranmer on the anniversary of his martyrdom" (http://listserv.virtueonline.org/pipermail/virtueonline_listserv.virtueonline.org/2002-March/003432.html; accessed May 10, 2011).

28 "Collect," *The Oxford Dictionary of the Christian Church*, ed. F.L. Cross and E.A. Livingstone, 3rd ed. (Oxford: Oxford University Press, 1997), 375–376.

Thomas Cranmer
1489–1556

marked by brevity and unity of thought. In the Anglican tradition as crafted by Cranmer, they generally have five parts. They normally invoke God the Father, though some call upon the Lord Jesus. There then follows a clause which makes mention of a divine attribute. There is a specific petition or two. Generally following the petition(s) is the purpose for which petition is made. Concluding the collect is an ascription of honour to Christ whose merits alone can obtain an answer to the request of his people.[29] Of the seventy collects in the 1552 *The Book of Common Prayer* Cranmer himself wrote about twenty-four collects, which are rightly described as "remarkable pieces of devotion."[30]

Here, for example, is the collect to be prayed on the second Sunday in Advent.

> Blessed lord, which hast caused all holy Scriptures to be written for our learning; grant us that we may in such wise hear them, read, mark, learn, and inwardly digest them; that by patience, and comfort of thy holy word, we may embrace, and ever hold fast the blessed hope of everlasting life, which thou hast given us in our saviour Jesus Christ.[31]

Cranmer's stress in this collect is a major aspect of his thinking about Holy Scripture, namely its utterly vital importance as a touchstone of truth and wisdom as well as its unique usefulness as a means of grace. Here, those who came to worship in the Reformed Church of England were being invited to learn the Bible and meditate on its life-giving riches, that they might derive from this meditative reading the patience and comfort, ie. strength, to embrace God's salvation in Christ. As Cranmer declared elsewhere:

---

29 Brooks, *Cranmer in Context*, 57–58; D.E.W. Harrison, *The Book of Common Prayer. The Anglican Heritage of Public Worship* (London/Edinburgh: Canterbury Press, 1946), 99–100. MacCulloch (*Thomas Cranmer*, 417) refers to them as "these jewelled miniatures [that] are one of the chief glories" of Anglican worship.

30 Brooks, *Cranmer in Context*, 58. For easy access to these collects, see C. Frederick Barbee and Paul F.M. Zahl, compiled, *The Collects of Thomas Cranmer* (Grand Rapids/Cambridge: William B. Eerdmans Publ. Co., 1999).

31 Barbee and Zahl, compiled, *Collects of Thomas Cranmer*, 4.

Dost thou not mark and consider how the smith, mason, or carpenter or any other handy-craftsman, what need soever he be in, …he will not sell nor lay to pledge the tools of his occupation, …for then how should he get a living thereby? Of like mind and affection ought we to be towards holy scripture. For as mallets, hammers, saws, chisels, axes and hatchets be the tools of their occupation, so be the books of the prophets and apostles, and all holy writ inspired by the Holy Ghost the instrument of our salvation.[32]

This explains Cranmer's efforts for much of his time as Archbishop of Canterbury to get the English Bible into the hands of the common person in England. As J.I. Packer rightly points out in this regard: "To make the Church of England a Bible-reading, Bible-loving church was Cranmer's constant ideal."[33] The ultimate fruit of this Bible-reading, Bible-loving church was Puritanism, and, of deep interest to this writer, the Calvinistic Baptist movement.

Or consider this portion of a prayer from the communion service in which Cranmer trumpets forth that salvation is by Christ alone:

Almighty God our heavenly Father, which of thy tender mercy didst give thine only Son Jesus Christ, to suffer death upon the cross for our redemption, who made there (by his one oblation of himself once offered) a full, perfect and sufficient sacrifice, oblation, and satisfaction, for the sins of the whole world, and did institute, and in his holy Gospel command us to continue, a perpetual memory of that his precious death, until his coming again; hear us O merciful Father we beseech thee…[34]

The declaration that Christ's death is "a full, perfect and sufficient

---

32 Quoted Samuel Leuenberger, *Archbishop Cranmer's Immortal Bequest: The Book of Common Prayer of the Church of England: An Evangelistic Liturgy*, trans. Samuel Leuenberger and Lewis J. Gorin, Jr. (Grand Rapids: William B. Eerdmans Publ. Co., 1990), 89.

33 "Thomas Cranmer's Catholic Theology" in his *Honouring the People of God*, 250.

34 *The First and Second Prayer Books of King Edward the Sixth* (London/Toronto: J.M. Dent & Sons/New York: E.P. Dutton, 1910), 389, alt. I have modernized the language.

sacrifice, oblation, and satisfaction" for sin undercuts the entire theological edifice of mediæval Roman Catholicism. For that edifice—with its understanding of the mass as a re-sacrifice for sin, both that of the living and that of the dead in purgatory, with its indulgences and rosaries and pilgrimages—was built on the supposition that humanity can do something to earn salvation. But Cranmer was convinced that all human endeavours to make appeasement for our sins and gain merit in the eyes of God are utterly futile. Due to the fact that, in Cranmer's words elsewhere, "all men be sinners and offenders against God, and breakers of his law and commandments, therefore can no man by his own acts, works, and deeds...be justified and made righteous before God."[35] Christ's peerless death is alone sufficient to appease the wrath of God against human sin and cleanse those who put their trust in him from all unrighteouness.[36]

Little wonder then that Cranmer was of the conviction that salvation by Christ alone and justification by faith alone

is the strong rock and foundation of Christian religion: this doctrine all old and ancient authors of Christ's Church do approve: this doctrine advanceth and setteth forth the true glory of Christ, and suppresseth the vainglory of man: this whosoever denieth is not to be reputed for a Christian man, nor for a setter forth of Christ's glory, but for an adversary to Christ and his gospel, and for a setter forth of men's vainglory.[37]

Here Cranmer identified what lay at the heart of the Reformation. The one side relied solely on the all-sufficiency of Christ's death—"a setter

---

35 *Homily of the Salvation of Mankind* in Parker, ed., *English Reformers*, 262.

36 For a good statement by Cranmer of his understanding of the doctrine of justification, see *Homily of the Salvation of Mankind* in Parker, ed., *English Reformers*, 262–272. For reflection on Cranmer's view, see Philip Edgcumbe Hughes, *Faith and Works: Cranmer and Hooker on Justification* (Wilton, Connecticut: Morehouse-Barlow Co., Inc., 1982); Packer, "Thomas Cranmer's Catholic Theology" in his *Honouring the People of God*, 250–254, 256; Alan C. Clifford, "Cranmer's Doctrine of Justification," *The Banner of Truth*, 315 (December 1989): 23–26; MacCulloch, *Thomas Cranmer*, 209–213, 341–347.

37 *Homily of the Salvation of Mankind* in Parker, ed., *English Reformers*, 266–267.

forth of Christ's glory" he calls each individual in this camp. The other side, which denied this biblical truth, Cranmer is convinced cannot be described as Christian, but must be seen as opposed to Christ and "a setter forth of men's vainglory." Within a year or so of the publication of the 1552 edition of the *Book of Common Prayer* the unbridgeable gulf between these two sides would plunge England, and Cranmer personally, into turmoil and bloody strife.

QUEEN MARY I AND ENGLAND'S "REIGN OF TERROR"

Edward VI died in 1553 of what is usually regarded as tuberculosis, though some recent scholarship as argued that he died of bronchopneumonia and that this had led to septicæmia.[38] Before his death, it is now clear that he sought to ensure that the Reformation that his reign had initiated would survive.[39] He thus changed the order of succession, away from both his half-sisters, Mary and Elizabeth, to a cousin, Lady Jane Grey (1537–1554), the grand-daughter of Henry VIII's sister Mary. For nine days after the death of Edward, Jane was queen. But Edward's "dreams of founding an evangelical realm of Christ" foundered and his sister Mary seized power in a *coup d'état* and began to reign as Mary I.[40]

Mary had been raised a fervent Roman Catholic, and she passionately believed that if she eliminated the core leadership of the evangelicals, the rest of England would docilely follow her back into the embrace of the Roman Church. She was wrong. Estimates as to how many were burned vary. Recent studies have identified 283 who were martyred. They range from bishops to brewers and barbers, from prominent preachers to teenage girls.[41] Her brutal persecution—for which there was no precedent in England—ultimately discredited Roman Catholicism, and when she died in 1558 of ovarian cancer, and her Protestant half-sister Elizabeth came to the throne, there was no popular regret at the realm becoming Protestant.

---

38 MacCulloch, *Tudor Church Militant*, 223–224, n.7.

39 MacCulloch, *Tudor Church Militant*, 39–41.

40 MacCulloch, *Tudor Church Militant*, 41. For a recent biography of Jane Grey, see Faith Cook, *Lady Jane Grey: Nine Day Queen of England* (Darlington: Evangelical Press, 2004).

41 For a recent account of these martyrs, see Andrew Atherstone, *The Martyrs of Mary Tudor* (Leominster: Day One, 2005).

"GOD...GRANT THAT I MAY ENDURE TO THE END"

Now, Cranmer had signed Edward's "devise for the succession," which placed Lady Jane Grey ever so briefly on the throne. Mary was determined he would pay for this and also for his role in her father's divorce of her mother. Mary allowed Cranmer to give Edward a Protestant funeral,[42] but once that had been done, he was arrested. The charge for his arrest was based on his involvement in the proclamation of Jane Grey as queen. He was sent to the Tower of London on September 13, 1553. Two months later he was tried for treason and convicted.[43] Mary loathed him, and there was no possibility of a reprieve. He spent six months in the Tower of London, and then, in April 1554, was taken to Oxford where he was submitted to a mock six-hour debate, in the Church of St. Mary the Virgin, where he had little real opportunity to defend his views.

Even though Cranmer had been convicted, he languished in Oxford's Bocardo prison, because ultimately only the pope could pass sentence on Cranmer, since his appointment as archbishop had been a papal one. It was thus not until September 1555 that Cranmer faced trial with a papal representative in England. The trial was designed to secure Cranmer's admission of guilt and give him no opportunity to defend his views. The trial devastated Cranmer. On December 4, 1555, Cranmer was formally excommunicated by Pope Paul IV (1476–1559).

Adding to his depression was the martyrdom of two of Cranmer's fellow bishops, Hugh Latimer and Nicholas Ridley (c.1500–1555). They were burned at the stake on October 16, 1555, in what is now Broad Street, Oxford, where a cross-shaped marker in the road today identifies their place of death. It was on this occasion that Latimer uttered those well-known words: "Be of good comfort, Master Ridley, and play the man! We shall this day light such a candle, by God's grace, in England, as I trust shall never be put out." Latimer died fairly swiftly, but the burning of Ridley was, to use the words of Peter Brooks, "an unusually vile affair," for the wood piled around him was freshly cut and thus only smouldered. He was in conscious agony till the very end

---

42 Brooks, *Cranmer in Context*, 89–90.

43 For a detailed account of Cranmer's trial, condemnation, imprisonment, and subsequent martyrdom, see MacCulloch, *Thomas Cranmer*, 554–605.

and at one point was heard to pray: "I cannot burn! Lord have mercy upon me!" Cranmer was compelled to watch their deaths from the roof of the Bocardo prison.[44]

Meanwhile Cranmer was tortured and forced to undergo what today we would call brainwashing sessions at the hands of a Spanish friar, Juan de Villa Garcia.[45] By such means, a recantation was obtained that completely repudiated the theology of the Reformation that had motivated Cranmer as a Reformer. It was probably Villa Garcia who wrote the recantation and had Cranmer sign it.[46] "I, Thomas Cranmer," the recantation read,

> anathematize every heresy of Luther and Zwingli...I confess and believe most surely in one holy and catholic visible church, outside which there is no salvation; and I recognize as its supreme head upon earth the Bishop of Rome, whom I admit to be *summus pontifex*, Pope and Vicar of Christ, to whom all the faithful are bound subject. Now as regards the sacraments, I believe in and worship in the sacrament of the Eucharist the true body and blood of Christ, most truly without recourse to any trope or figure of speech contained under the species of bread and wine, the bread being changed and transubstantiated by divine power into the Redeemer's body, and wine into his blood. And I believe in the other six sacraments...and hold that which the whole Roman church holds and declares."[47]

Another recantation was to follow in which he asked forgiveness for what he done against the realm of England by being the "cause and originator" of Henry's divorce of Catherine of Aragon, which was confessed to be the seed-bed for all that followed in Henry's reign, the bloodshed and emergence of heresy.[48] These private recantations,

---

44 Brooks, *Cranmer in Context*, 93–94; Atherstone, *The Martyrs of Mary Tudor*, 93–99; David Horan, *Oxford: A cultural and literary companion* (New York/Northampton: Interlink Books, 2000), 129–130.

45 Brooks, *Cranmer in Context*, 97–98.

46 MacCulloch, *Thomas Cranmer*, 594–595.

47 Cited Brooks, *Cranmer in Context*, 112.

48 Brooks, *Cranmer in Context*, 113–115; MacCulloch, *Thomas Cranmer*, 598–599.

though, were not enough for the authorities. Cranmer was informed that he would have to give a public recantation on the day of his being burnt by fire on Saturday, March 21, 1556.

That Saturday it was a cold, wet, windy March morning. Cranmer was taken from the Bocardo prison to the Church of St. Mary the Virgin where he was placed on a raised platform in the full view of all who were there. He was once again berated for his heresies and then given the opportunity to speak where it was expected that he would repeat his earlier recantations. But by God's grace he was enabled to speak what he truly believed.

Cranmer began with a prayer in which he confessed his sins and expressed his confidence in God's mercy.[49] Then followed what was expected to be his public recantation. It began with exhortations to the audience and included one to obey "your King and Queen, willingly and gladly, without murmuring or grudging,"[50] but it ended in a way that was utterly unexpected.

> And now, for so much as I am come to the last end of my life, whereupon hangeth all my life passed, and my life to come, either to live with my master Christ for ever in joy, or else to be in pain for ever, with wicked devils in hell; and I see before mine eyes presently either heaven ready to receive me, or hell ready to swallow me up: I shall therefore declare unto you my very faith, how I believe, without any colour or dissimulation: for now is no time to dissemble, whatsoever I have said or written in times past.[51]

After stating his belief in "every article of the Catholic faith" and "every word and sentence taught" in the Scriptures he continued, though

---

49 *The Works of Thomas Cranmer*, ed. G.E. Duffield (Appleford: Sutton Courtenay Press, 1964), 334–335. For a study of Cranmer's martyrdom, see Rudolph W. Heinze, "'I pray God to grant that I may endure to the end': A New Look at the Martyrdom of Thomas Cranmer" in Paul Ayris and David Selwyn, eds., *Thomas Cranmer: Churchman and Scholar* (Woodbridge: Boydell Press, 1993), 278–279.

50 *Works of Thomas Cranmer*, 335.

51 *Works of Thomas Cranmer*, 337.

deadly pale, but with, as MacCulloch puts it, "a surge of energy"[52]:

> And now I come to the great thing that so much troubleth my
> conscience, more than any thing that ever I did or said in my whole
> life: and that is, the setting abroad of writings contrary to the truth;
> which now here I renounce and refuse, as things written with my
> hand, contrary to the truth which I thought in my heart, and writ-
> ten for fear of death, and to save my life, if it might be; and that is,
> all such bills, which I have written or signed with my hand since
> my degradation: wherein I have written many things untrue. And
> forasmuch as my hand offended, writing contrary to my heart,
> my hand shall first be punished therefore; for, may I come to the
> fire, it shall be first burned. And as for the Pope, I refuse him, as
> Christ's enemy and Antichrist, with all his false doctrine....[53]

Amidst much yelling that this was not his signed recantation, he was
pulled down from the platform on which he had been standing. He
responded, "always since I lived, ...I have been a hater of falsehood,
and a lover of simplicity, and never, before this time, have I dissembled,"
and he began to cry.[54] He then literally ran to the stake in what is now
Broad Street with the Spanish friar Villa Garcia running after him
trying to get him to recant once again. The Spanish friar continued
trying to get him to recant all the way to the stake, but Cranmer was
steadfast. In fact, when he was chained to the stake and the wood set
on fire, he stretched out his arm, and, we are told,

> put his right hand into the flame, which he held so steadfast and
> immoveable...that all men might see his hand burned before his
> body was touched....oftentimes he repeated, his unworthy right
> hand, so long as his voice would suffer him; and using often the
> words of Stephen, "Lord Jesus, receive my spirit," in the greatness
> of the flame he gave up the ghost.[55]

---

52 MacCulloch, *Thomas Cranmer*, 603.
53 *Works of Thomas Cranmer*, 337–338.
54 *Works of Thomas Cranmer*, 338.
55 *Works of Thomas Cranmer*, 339–340.

A few months before his martyrdom, Cranmer had written a letter to Peter Martyr—it may well have been the last letter he ever wrote.

God never shines forth more brightly, and pours out the beams of his mercy and consolation, or of strength and firmness of spirit more clearly or impressively upon the minds of his people, than when they are under the most extreme pain and distress, both of mind and body, that he may then more especially shew himself to be the God of his people, when he seems to have altogether forsaken them; then raising them up when they think he is bringing them down, and laying them low; then glorifying them, when he is thought to be confounding them; then quickening them, when he is thought to be destroying them. So that we may say with Paul, "When I am weak, then am I strong; and if I must needs glory, I will glory in my infirmities, in prisons, in revilings, in distresses, in persecutions, in sufferings for Christ." I pray God to grant that I may endure to the end.[56]

God gave him the enduring grace for which he prayed.

The account of Cranmer's martyrdom is not one of unbroken triumph, but, of victory being snatched out of the jaws of defeat. In some respects, Cranmer appears a very ordinary man, one with no taste for violent death. But in his final hours God's grace enabled him to endure to the end, and we see that what Cranmer had taught as an evangelical—namely, that salvation is wholly the Lord's work—is shown to be true in his final hours.[57]

---

56 Heinze, "New Look at the Martyrdom of Thomas Cranmer," 277.
57 Bromiley, "Thomas W. Cranmer," 188.

4

"Uttering the praises of the Father, of the Son, and of the Spirit"

John Calvin on the Holy Trinity

It is impossible to praise God without also uttering the praises of the Father, of the Son, and of the Spirit.
—JOHN CALVIN[1]

In a masterful study of the unfolding of early Christian thought, Jarolsav Pelikan, the doyen of twentieth-century Patristic studies, noted that the "climax of the doctrinal development of the early church was the

---

1   John Calvin, *Commentary on Isaiah 6:2*, vol. 1, *Commentary on the Book of the Prophet Isaiah*, trans. William Pringle (Reprint, Grand Rapids: Baker Book House, 1989), 205.

dogma of the Trinity."[2] And the textual expression of that climax is undoubtedly the Niceno-Constantinopolitan Creed that was issued at the Council of Constantinople (A.D. 381), in which Jesus Christ is unequivocally declared to be "true God" and "of one being (*homoousios*) with the Father," and the Holy Spirit is described as the "Lord and Giver of life," who "together with the Father and the Son is worshipped and glorified." The original Nicene Creed, issued by the Council of Nicaea in A.D. 325, had made a similar statement about the Son and his deity, but nothing had been said about the Holy Spirit beyond the statement "[We believe] in the Holy Spirit." When the deity of the Spirit was subsequently questioned in the 360s and 370s, it was necessary to expand the Nicene Creed to include a statement about the deity of the Holy Spirit. In the end, this expansion involved the drafting of a new creedal statement at the Council of Constantinople.[3]

THE SERVETUS AFFAIR

Apart from the controversy between the Greek East and the Latin West over the *filioque*, the Niceno-Constantinopolitan creed essentially closed the door on debates about the Trinity for the next millennium. With the upheaval, however, caused by the Reformers' questions about salvation, worship and the source of authority, it is not surprising that some would broach questions about Trinitarian matters long thought settled.

On three distinct occasions, for instance, John Calvin found himself embroiled in controversy about the triune nature of God. One is all

---

2   *The Christian Tradition: Vol. 1: The Emergence of the Catholic Tradition (100-600)* (Chicago/London: The University of Chicago Press, 1971), 172. For help in locating sources for this chapter, I am indebted to my colleague, Dr. David Puckett of The Southern Baptist Theological Seminary, and my assistant at the Andrew Fuller Center for Baptist Studies, Rev. Steve Weaver. This chapter was originally given as a paper at the «Cinquième centenaire de Jean Calvin: La Réforme francophone en milieu qué-bécois, un demi-millénaire plus tard», held on October 23–24, 2009 at Farel Reformed Theological Seminary, Montreal.

3   For the text of these two creeds, see J.N.D. Kelly, *Early Christian Creeds*, 2nd ed. (London: Longmans, Green and Co. Ltd., 1960), 215–216, 297–298. See also Johannes Roldanus, *The Church in the Age of Constantine: The theological challenges* (Abingdon/New York: Routledge, 2006), 123–126.

too well known, namely, the controversy with the Spanish humanist and physician Michael Servetus (1511–1553), whose execution in Geneva on October 27, 1553, has defined, for many, Calvin's character as a theocratic tyrant.[4] Servetus had been incessant in his rejection of the ontological deity of Christ and in his anti-Trinitarian campaigning, even daring to call the blessed Trinity a "hell's dog with three heads, [a] devilish phantom" and "an illusion of Satan."[5] He also appears to have been obsessed with coming to Geneva to finally confront the man he regarded as the arch-enemy of the true Reformation.[6] For his part, Calvin viewed Servetus as a very dangerous heretic. Yet, while the French Reformer did play a role in Servetus' condemnation, Calvin's Geneva was not a theocracy by any stretch of the imagination.[7] Moreover, at the time of Servetus' execution Calvin did not have the political power to sentence anyone to death, and those who condemned Servetus in this regard were actually Calvin's opponents, who used the occasion to assert their authority over the French Reformer.[8] Nevertheless, as Sebastian Castellio (1515–1563), a one-time co-worker of Calvin who later became one of his most ardent opponents, observed in a work that he wrote against Calvin's 1554 defence of the heretic's execution:

To kill a man is not to protect a doctrine, but it is to kill a man. When the Genevans killed Servetus, they did not defend a doctrine,

---

4   Bruce Gordon, *Calvin* (New Haven/London: Yale University Press, 2009), 217. On Calvin's controversy with Servetus, see Eric Kayam, "The Case of Michael Servetus: The background and unfolding of the case," *Mid-America Journal of Theology*, 8, no.2 (Fall 1992): 117–146; Gordon, *Calvin*, 217–232; Jean-Luc Mouton, *Calvin* ([Paris]: Éditions Gallimard, 2009), 302–342; Christoph Strohm, "Calvin and Religious Tolerance," trans. David Dichelle in Martin Ernst Hirzel and Martin Sallmann, ed., *John Calvin's Impact on Church and Society, 1509–2009* (Grand Rapids/Cambridge: William B. Eerdmans Publ. Co., 2009), 176–179.

5   Cited Kayam, "Case of Michael Servetus," 123.

6   Gordon, *Calvin*, 218–219.

7   On Geneva not being a theocracy, see Mark J. Larson, *Calvin's Doctrine of the State* (Eugene: Wipf & Stock, 2009), 1–19.

8   J.I. Packer, "John Calvin and Reformed Europe" in John D. Woodbridge, ed., *Great Leaders of the Christian Church* (Chicago: Moody Press, 1988), 212–213; Gordon, *Calvin*, 217–229.

they killed a man. To protect a doctrine is not the magistrate's affair (what has the sword to do with doctrine?) but the teacher's....But when Servetus fought with reasons and writings, he should have been repulsed by reasons and writings.[9]

THE CONTROVERSY WITH PIERRE CAROLI

Two decades before this controversy with Servetus, though, the shoe had been on the other foot, as Calvin, along with his close friends Guillaume Farel (1489–1565) and Pierre Viret (1511–1571), had been charged with Arianism by Pierre Caroli (c.1480–c.1547). Like Farel, Caroli had come from the circle of reform associated with Jacques Lefèvre d'Étaples (c.1455–1536), but, unlike Farel, Caroli never decisively committed himself to the theological agenda of the Reformation. A one-time professor of theology at the Sorbonne, Caroli had fled France in the 1530s after embracing Protestantism. He eventually made his way to Lausanne, where he was appointed the main preacher in the city. Caroli was theologically unstable, though, and returned to the Roman Church in the summer of 1537, only to leave that communion for Protestantism once again in 1539. Warfield has rightly described him as "one of the most frivolous characters brought to the surface by the upheaval of the Reformation."[10]

---

9   *Contra libellum Calvini in quo ostendere conatur haereticos jure gladii coercendos esse* (Holland, 1612). Though published in 1612, Castellio actually wrote this work in 1554 as a response to Calvin's *Defensio orthodoxae fidei de sacra Trinitate* (1554), his justification of the execution of Servetus. For the quote, I am indebted to "Sebastian Castellio and the Struggle for Freedom of Conscience" (http://www.socinian.org/castellio.html#_edn16; accessed October 20, 2009) and Timothy George, "Calvin's Biggest Mistake: Why he assented to the execution of Michael Servetus," *Christianity Today* 53, no. 9 (September 2009): 32. For an overview of Castellio's views on religious tolerance, see Strohm, "Calvin and Religious Tolerance," 187–188.

10   "Calvin's Doctrine of the Trinity" in his *Calvin and Augustine*, ed. Samuel G. Craig (Philadelphia: Presbyterian and Reformed Publishing Co., 1980), 204. For an extremely thorough overview of the so-called Caroli affair, see Karl Barth, *The Theology of John Calvin*, trans. Geoffrey W. Bromiley (Grand Rapids/Cambridge: William B. Eerdmans Pub. Co., 1995), 309–345. For the course of the affair, see also Warfield, "Calvin's Doctrine of the Trinity," 204–212; Richard C. Gamble, "Calvin's Controversies" in Donald K. McKim, ed., *The Cambridge Companion to John Calvin* (Cambridge: Cambridge University Press, 2004), 199; Gordon, *Calvin*, 72–75.

Caroli found ammunition for his charge against Calvin and his friends in the fact that Farel, in his *Sommaire et brève declaration* (1525), the first work in French to set forth the essential aspects of the Reformed faith, omitted any clear reference to the Trinity, as did the confession of faith drawn up in 1536 for the church in Geneva.[11] The emptiness of Caroli's accusation is immediately apparent, however, when one considers that in the first edition of Calvin's *Institutes*— published in Basel in March 1536, and available to Caroli before he made his accusation—the French Reformer had set forth a decisive rejection of Arianism and a clear affirmation of his belief in the Trinity:

> Persons who are not contentious or stubborn see the Father, Son, and Holy Spirit to be one God. For the Father is God; the Son is God; and the Spirit is God: and there can be only one God.
>
> On the other hand, three are named, three described, three distinguished. One therefore, and three: one God, one essence. Why three? Not three gods, not three essences. To signify both, the ancient orthodox fathers said that there was one *ousia*, three *hypostaseis*, that is, one substance, three subsistences in one substance.[12]

Here there is not only a solid declaration of the Trinity, but Calvin is also quite happy to express this declaration by means of non-biblical terms hammered out in the debates about the Trinity in the fourth century, namely *ousia* ("being") and *hypostasis* ("subsistence").

Caroli leveled his accusation against the French Reformers during a disputation between Calvin, Viret and himself at Lausanne on February 17, 1537, over the rectitude of praying for the dead.[13] Calvin's immediate response was to cite a catechism that was used in the church at Geneva, in which there was a brief statement of the triunity

---

11 Guillaume Farel, *Sommaire et brève declaration*, trans. and ed. Arthur L. Hofer (Neuchâtel: Éditions « Belle Rivière », 1980), 13–14.

12 *Institutes of the Christian Religion* 2.A.7, trans. Ford Lewis Battles, rev. ed. (Grand Rapids: H.H. Meeter Center for Calvin Studies/William B. Eerdmans Pub. Co., 1986), 45. For the rejection of Arianism, see *Institutes of the Christian Religion* 2.A.9 (47–48).

13 Barth, *Theology of John Calvin*, 317–318.

of God. It is noteworthy that he did not refer to the passage from his *Institutes* cited above. Caroli refused to consider the catechism to be an adequate expression of Trinitarian faith, and demanded that Calvin subscribe then and there to the time-honoured Athanasian Creed. Calvin refused to acquiesce to Caroli's demand, for, he explained, he was not prepared to regard any text as authoritative for doctrine unless it had first been tested against the Word of God. At this point, Caroli apparently became incensed and dramatically yelled back that Calvin's explanation was "unbecoming a Christian man."[14] Nearly ten years later, in his pseudonymous *Defence of Guillaume Farel and his colleagues against the calumnies of Pierre Caroli* (1545), Calvin was also somewhat critical of the format of another of the ancient church's creeds, the Nicene Creed, which, as has been noted above, was regarded as the definitive expression of Trinitarianism. Calvin felt that the creed contained needless repetition in clauses like "God of God, light of light, true God of true God." "Why this repetition?" he asked. "Does it add any more emphasis or greater expression? You see, therefore, it is a song, more to be sung, than a suitable rule of faith, in which one redundant syllable is absurd."[15]

Not surprisingly, such statements gave substance to Caroli's accusations, and the suspicion that Calvin was unsound regarding Trinitarian doctrine dogged him for years to come.[16] But Calvin was unwilling to have his faith confined to the exact wording of the ancient church's creeds. The touchstone of Scripture was alone requisite in deciding

---

14 Letter to Kaspar Megander [February, 1537] in John Calvin, *Tracts and Letters*, ed. Jules Bonnet and trans. David Constable (1858; reprint, Edinburgh/Carlisle: The Banner of Truth Trust, 2009), 4:49.

15 *Pro G. Farello et collegis eius adversus Petri Caroli calumnias defensio Nicolai Gallasii* in *Ioannis Calvini opera quae supersunt omnia*, ed. Wilhelm Baum, Eduard Cunitz and Eduard Reuss (Brunswick: C.A. Schwetschke and Son, 1868; reprint, New York/London: Johnson Reprint Corp./Frankfurt am Main: Minerva, G.m.b.H, 1964), 7:315–316, trans. author. Henceforth the works of Calvin will be designated as *Calvini opera* with the appropriate volume and column.

16 A. Mitchell Hunter, *The Teaching of Calvin. A Modern Interpretation*, 2nd ed. (London: James Clarke & Co., 1950), 42–43; Bernard Cottret, *Calvin. A Biography*, trans. M. Wallace McDonald (Grand Rapids/Cambridge: William B. Eerdmans Pub. Co./Edinburgh: T&T Clark, 2000), 124–126.

between what was orthodox and what was not.[17] On the other hand, Calvin was equally insistent in the course and aftermath of the Caroli affair that he and his colleagues were fully committed to orthodox Trinitarianism. At a synod that was convened in the Franciscan church in Lausanne on May 14, 1537, to settle the Caroli controversy, Viret spoke for Calvin and Farel when he stated that:

> We confess one God, in one essence of divinity (*sub una divinitatis essentia*), and we hold together the Father with his eternal Word and Spirit. We thus call the Father God in such a way that we proclaim the Son and his Spirit to be the true and eternal God with the Father. We neither confuse the Father with the Word, nor the Word with the Spirit. For we believe the Son to be other than the Father, and again the Spirit to differ from the Son, although there is [only] one [divine] being.[18]

What is noteworthy about this confession is that it is not only an unambiguous rejection of Arianism, but it also avoids another bugbear of the ancient church, namely Sabellianism or modalism.[19]

The Caroli controversy reveals Calvin to have been thoroughly convinced that one must reverently accept the triunity of God as fully biblical, but also determined to maintain an independence of the wording of the Patristic creeds.[20] In the words of Arie Baars, Calvin "strongly opposes any theology that is characterized by a speculative... inquisitiveness that does not respect the boundaries of Scripture."[21] Thus, in his conflict with Caroli, Calvin made little use of the Patristic way of distinguishing the hypostatic differences within the Trinity, namely, that the Son is eternally begotten of the Father and that the

---

17 Warfield, "Calvin's Doctrine of the Trinity," 207–211; Hunter, *Teaching of Calvin*, 45–48.

18 *Pro G. Farello...defensio* (*Calvini opera*, 7:312), trans. author.

19 Barth, *Theology of John Calvin*, 324–325.

20 Hunter, *Teaching of Calvin*, 41; Stephen M. Reynolds, "Calvin's View of the Athanasian and Nicene Creeds," *The Westminster Theological Journal*, 23 (1960–1961): 33–37.

21 Arie Baars, "The Trinity," trans. Gerrit W. Sheeres in Herman J. Selderhuis, ed., *The Calvin Handbook* (Grand Rapids/Cambridge: William B. Eerdmans Pub. Co., 2009), 246.

Spirit eternally proceeds from the Father and the Son.[22] But Calvin was determined to uphold the Trinitarianism of the ancient church and showed a willingness at times, as the first edition of the *Institutes* shows, to use extra-biblical terms to clarify scriptural truth.[23]

THE BATTLE WITH THE ITALIAN ANTI-TRINITARIANS

Controversy with anti-Trinitarianism in the 1550s, that of Michael Servetus earlier in the decade and then that of various Italian Protestants in the latter part of the decade, forced Calvin to develop a more explicit and detailed Trinitarianism, which is evident in the final edition of the *Institutes* (1559).[24] An Italian congregation had been meeting for regular worship in Geneva since 1542, but when their minister Celso Martinengo (1515–1557) died in the summer of 1557, the community was wracked by quarrels over the doctrine of the Trinity. One of the instigators of these theological quarrels was Matteo Gribaldi (c.1505–1564), who had taught law at the University of Padua before taking up a position at the university in Tübingen.[25] Gribaldi had been in Geneva at the outset of the trial of Servetus and had taken the heretic's side though his own conviction about the Godhead appears to have been tritheistic.[26] Gribaldi's opposition to orthodox Trinitarianism subsequently had a major influence over a number of the members of the Genevan Italian community, including Giorgio Biandrata (1516–1588),[27] Giovanni Alciati (c.1515/1520–1573) and Valentino

---

22 Paul Helm, *Calvin: A Guide for the Perplexed* (London/New York: T&T Clark, 2008), 44.

23 Baars, "Trinity," 245–246; Helm, *Calvin*, 41–44.

24 Helm, *Calvin*, 44–45.

25 On Gribaldi, see James T. Dennison, Jr., and George C. Young II with Francis X. Gumerlock and Andrea Rafanelli, "Trinitarian Confession of the Italian Church of Geneva (1558)," *Kerux* 21, no.1 (May 2006): 3–4 and n.4; Peter Hughes, "Matteo Gribaldi" (http://www25-temp.uua.org/uuhs/duub/articles/matteogribaldi.html; accessed October 21, 2009).

26 Dennison, Jr., and Young II with Gumerlock and Rafanelli, "Trinitarian Confession of the Italian Church," 4, n.4.

27 On Biandrata, see Joseph N. Tylenda, "The warning that went unheeded: John Calvin on Giorgio Binadrata," *Calvin Theological Journal*, 12 (April–November 1977): 24–62; Charles A. Howe and Peter Huges, "George Biandrata" (http://www25.uua.org/uuhs/duub/articles/giorgiobiandrata.html; accessed October 21, 2009).

Gentile (c.1520–1566), from Calabria, who began to voice their views in the course of 1557 and 1558.

Biandrata, for example, argued that "Jesus never revealed to the world a God other than his Father." In his teaching, Jesus never once taught about God being "one essence in three persons," something that Biandrata deemed "clearly incomprehensible."[28] Gentile, on the other hand, argued that there are indeed three persons in the Godhead, but "only the Father is *autotheos*, that is, has his essence (*essentiatus*) from no superior deity, but is God of himself."[29] Neither the Son nor the Spirit are *autotheos*, for the Father poured, as it were, some of his divine being into them and thus deified them.[30]

Calvin responded to these arguments through a number of written texts as well as personal meetings with the Italians.[31] From New Testament texts like Romans 9:5; John 1:1; 20:28 and 2 Corinthians 12:8–9, Calvin can only conclude that Jesus is recognized to be fully God by the New Testament authors.[32] And to Biandrata's argument that "the one essence in three persons was not revealed by Christ," Calvin responded by referring, among other things, to the baptismal command of Matthew 28:19 where Christ "distinctly and undeniably named...[the] three persons of the Father, and of the Son, and of the Holy Spirit."[33] This appeal to Scripture reflected Calvin's conviction that theological reflection about "the one essence and the three persons" is not a waste of time, for the scriptural witness about God

---

28 Tylenda, "The warning that went unheeded," 52–53.

29 *Impietas Valentini Gentilis detecta et palam traducta, qui Christum non sine sacrilega blasphemia Deum essentiatum esse fingit* (1561) (*Calvini opera* 9:374).

30 *Institutes* 1.13.23–26. See also Thomas F. Torrance, "Calvin's Doctrine of the Trinity," *Calvin Theological Journal*, 25, no. 2 (November 1990): 180–181; Robert Letham, *The Holy Trinity In Scripture, History, Theology, and Worship* (Phillipsburg: Presbyterian and Reformed Publishing Co., 2004), 256; Baars, "The Trinity," 250.

31 See, for example, John Calvin, *Ad quaestiones Georgii Blandratae responsum* (1558) (*Calvini opera* 9:321–332); "Confession of Faith set forth in the Italian Church of Geneva May 18, 1558" (Dennison, Jr., and Young II with Gumerlock and Rafanelli, "Trinitarian Confession of the Italian Church," 6–10); *Impietas Valentini Gentilis* (*Calvini opera* 9:361–420).

32 *Ad quaestiones Georgii Blandratae responsum* (1558) (*Calvini opera* 9:327–329).

33 *Ad quaestiones Georgii Blandratae responsum* (1558) (*Calvini opera* 9:328) (trans. Tylenda, "The warning that went unheeded," 58).

clearly proceeds from the presupposition of the Trinity.[34] In fact, at the close of his brief reply to Biandrata, Calvin appealed to the Nicene Creed and the writings of "Athanasius and other ancients," which, according to his reading of their texts, affirmed that though "the Son is distinct from the Father, nevertheless, he is true God, and the same God with him, except in what pertains to his person" and that there are "three coeternal [persons] but nevertheless one eternal God."[35]

In May 1558, Calvin helped to draw up a Trinitarian confession of faith for the Italian church in which the errors of Gentile were specifically condemned: "whatever is attributed" to the Father's "deity, glory and essence, is suitable as much to the Son as to the Holy Spirit."[36] It is noteworthy that in this confession, Calvin uses the classical concepts of eternal generation and eternal procession to distinguish the Father from the Son and the Spirit. In his words:

> we profess God the Father even to have begotten his Word or Wisdom from eternity, who is his only Son, and the Holy Spirit thus to have proceeded from them both since there is one sole essence of the Father, Son, and Holy Spirit.[37]

In Calvin's main response to the arguments of these heterodox Italians, namely, the fifth edition of his *Institutes* (1559), Calvin employs Scripture to demonstrate the consubstantiality of the Father with both the Son and the Spirit.[38] And because Gentile also argued for his position from the writings of the second-century Fathers, Irenaeus of Lyons (c.130–c.200) and Tertullian (fl.190–220),[39] Calvin sought to

---

34 *Ad quaestiones Georgii Blandratae responsum* (1558) (*Calvini opera* 9:331).

35 *Ad quaestiones Georgii Blandratae responsum* (1558) (*Calvini opera* 9:331–332) (trans. Tylenda, "The warning that went unheeded," 61–62).

36 "Confession of Faith set forth in the Italian Church of Geneva May 18, 1558" (Dennison, Jr., and Young II with Gumerlock and Rafanelli, "Trinitarian Confession of the Italian Church," 9).

37 "Confession of Faith set forth in the Italian Church of Geneva May 18, 1558" (Dennison, Jr., and Young II with Gumerlock and Rafanelli, "Trinitarian Confession of the Italian Church," 8).

38 *Institutes* 1.13.23–25.

39 *Impietas Valentini Gentilis* (*Calvini opera* 9:394–396).

John Calvin
1509–1564

Credit: Translation of the inscription: John Calvin of Noyon in Picardy, Pastor of the Church of Geneva. From "The Medals of Calvin" in John Calvin, Commentaries on the First Book of Moses called Genesis, trans. John King (Edinburgh: Calvin Translation Society, 1847).

show that neither of these Patristic authors, properly interpreted, supported Gentile's position.[40] In fact, Calvin is confident that his own Trinitarian perspective is in complete harmony with that of the ancient church.[41]

THE FATHERS AS CONVERSATION PARTNERS[42]

Calvin can be critical of the Church Fathers, but those occasions occur mostly in his exegetical commentaries, and then, in relation to the Fathers' unwarranted use of biblical texts to support their dogmatic statements.[43] In his 1548 commentary on Colossians, for instance, Calvin notes the fact that "the old writers" during the Arian controversy employed Colossians 1:15 to "emphasize the equality of the Son with the Father" and to assert the Nicene watchword, the consubstantiality (*homoousia*) of the Father and the Son.[44] One of the "old writers" that Calvin has in mind was John Chrysostom (c.347–407), the one-time Patriarch of Constantinople. According to Calvin, Chrysostom argued that the word "image" speaks of Christ's divine status, since "the creature cannot be said to be the image of the Creator." Calvin, though, found this to be a very weak argument, since Paul can use the very word "image" of human beings, as, for example, in 1 Corinthians 11:7, where Paul says man is "the image and glory of God." The word "image," Calvin points out, does not refer to Christ's essence, but is being used as an epistemological term. Christ is "the image of God because he makes God, in a manner, visible to us." He can only do so, Calvin avers, because he is "the essential Word of God" and consubstantial with the Father. Behind this affirmation lies a key principle that Calvin has drawn from his reading of the Church Fathers: only God can reveal God. Colossians 1:15 therefore does speak of the Son's *homoousia* with the Father and is "a powerful weapon against the Arians." Calvin thus arrives at the same place as Chrysostom, but he does

---

40 *Institutes* 1.13.27–28.

41 *Institutes* 1.13.29.

42 This expression is that of Baars, "The Trinity," 247.

43 Baars, "The Trinity," 247.

44 Commentary on Colossians 1:15 in John Calvin, *The Epistles of Paul The Apostle to the Galatians, Ephesians, Philippians and Colossians*, trans. T.H.L. Parker, *Calvin's Commentaries* (Edinburgh/London: Oliver and Boyd, 1965), 308.

so by a more rigorous hermeneutic that pays proper attention to the text. Calvin concludes that this text is a good reminder that "God in himself, that is, in his naked majesty" is invisible to both the physical eye and the eye of human understanding. Only in Christ is God revealed. To seek God elsewhere is to engage in idolatry.

A second example in which Calvin engages Patristic Trinitarian exegesis is his commentary on Hebrews 1:2–3,[45] which the French Reformer wrote the year following his commentary on Colossians. Hebrews 1 was regularly mined in the Patristic era for proof of Christ's divinity, and understandably so in light of its high Christology. Following in the train of this exegetical tradition, Calvin deduces the eternal nature of Christ from the fact that he made the world. Since the Father is usually identified as the Creator of the world, this means that there are at least two "persons" involved in this divine work. Since Calvin assumes only God can do such creative work, the Son must be fully divine and share a "unity of essence" with the Father. As persons they are to be distinguished, but as God they have in common "whatever belongs to God alone."

Hebrews 1:3 also speaks of the deity of Christ, though Calvin is careful to note at the outset of his commentary that the reader of Hebrews should not seek to investigate the "hidden majesty of God" by enquiring into the exact way "the Son, who is of one essence with the Father, is the glory shining forth from his brightness." By describing Christ in this way, the author of Hebrews is not seeking to depict "the likeness of the Father to the Son within the Godhead," for "God is incomprehensible to us in himself." Rather, this description is yet another vital reminder that "God is revealed to us in no other way than in Christ."

Hebrews 1:3 also states that Christ is "the very image" of the Father's "substance" (*hypostasis*). By *hypostasis*, Calvin understands the hypostatic distinctiveness of the Father, not the "essence of the Father." To make the latter point would be redundant, Calvin believes, since both

45 Commentary on Hebrews 1:2–3 in John Calvin, *The Epistle of Paul The Apostle to the Hebrews and The First and Second Epistles of St Peter*, trans. William B. Johnston, *Calvin's Commentaries* (1963 ed.; reprint, Grand Rapids: William B. Eerdmans Publ. Co./Carlisle: The Paternoster Press, 1994), 6–9.

the Father and the Son share the same essence. Calvin is conscious that his interpretation follows in the pathway of Patristic exegesis, for Latin exegetes like Hilary of Poitiers (c.300–c.368), a staunch opponent of Arianism, made the same point. In other words, Calvin is convinced that this clause declares that anything we know of the Father we find revealed in the person of Christ. While Paul's intention in this text is not to discuss Christ's divine being, which some of the Fathers might not have grasped, yet Calvin believes this clause "refutes the Arians and the Sabellians." It ascribes to Christ what belongs to God alone, namely the power to reveal God, and thus the reader is right to infer that "the Son is one God with the Father." At the same time it upholds the distinctiveness of the Father and the Son as persons.

Another key text used by Patristic authors like Athanasius (c.298–373) and Basil of Caesarea (c.329–379) to prove the deity of the Son and the Spirit was the baptismal formula in Matthew 28:19. Calvin likewise sees in this verse evidence of the triune nature of God.[46] Until the coming of Christ, "the full and clear knowledge" of God's nature remained hidden. While God's Old Covenant people had some knowledge of the wisdom and Spirit of God, it was only when the gospel began to be preached that "God was far more clearly revealed under three persons." Then "the Father showed himself in the Son, his living and express image, and Christ himself, by the brilliant light of his Spirit, shone out upon the world and held out himself and the Spirit to the minds of men."[47] Tying this Matthean verse to another Trinitarian text, Titus 3:5, Calvin concludes that there is a very good reason for Jesus to mention all three persons of the Godhead since there can be no saving knowledge of God "unless our faith distinctly conceives three persons in one essence."[48]

Finally, consider some of Calvin's exegetical remarks on the commissioning of the prophet in Isaiah 6. Calvin notes that verse 3 was

---

46 Commentary on Matthew 28:19 in Jean Calvin, *A Harmony of the Gospels, Matthew, Mark and Luke*, trans. A.W. Morrison (Grand Rapids: William B. Eerdmans Publ. Co., 1972), 3:253.

47 Commentary on Matthew 28:19 in Calvin, *Harmony of the Gospels*, trans. Morrison, 3:253, altered.

48 Commentary on Matthew 28:19 in *Harmony of the Gospels*, trans. Morrison, 3:253, altered.

often cited by the "ancients," that is, the Church Fathers, "when they wished to prove that there are three persons in one essence of the Godhead."[49] On one level Calvin does not disagree with this interpretation. He has no doubt that the angelic worship of God involves all three persons of the Godhead as "it is impossible to praise God without also uttering the praises of the Father, of the Son, and of the Spirit."[50] But, Calvin argues, there are much stronger passages to prove this article of the Christian faith. And he fears that the use of such "inconclusive" texts as this one will simply embolden the opposition of heretics. Calvin actually does find a good support for Trinitarianism a few verses later, when the question is asked by God, "Who will go for us?" Calvin believes that the use of the plural here, as in Genesis 1:26, unquestionably reflects the Father's consultation "with his eternal Wisdom and his eternal Power, that is, with the Son and the Holy Spirit."[51]

Finally, Calvin does not fail to reflect on the Trinitarian implications of the fact that the message given to Isaiah to deliver to Israel is twice cited in the New Testament. In the first citation in John 12:37–41, John states that when Isaiah heard these words he saw the glory of Christ. Then Paul cites this same passage as a word from the Holy Spirit (Acts 28:25–28). From these two New Testament citations of the Isaiah text, it is evident, Calvin argues, that:

> Christ was that God who filled the whole earth with his majesty. Now, Christ is not separate from his Spirit, and therefore Paul had good reason for applying this passage to the Holy Spirit; for although God exhibited to the Prophet the lively image of himself in Christ, still it is certain that whatever he communicated was wholly breathed into him by the power of the Holy Spirit.[52]

---

49 Commentary on Isaiah 6:3 in Commentary on the Book of the Prophet Isaiah, trans. William Pringle (Reprint, Grand Rapids: Baker Book House, 1989), 1:205.

50 Commentary on Isaiah 6:3 in Commentary on the Book of the Prophet Isaiah, trans. Pringle, 1:205.

51 Commentary on Isaiah 6:8 in Commentary on the Book of the Prophet Isaiah, trans. Pringle, 1:213.

52 Commentary on Isaiah 6:10 in Commentary on the Book of the Prophet Isaiah, trans. Pringle, 1:218–219.

A CONCLUDING WORD

From Calvin's response to Pierre Caroli's charges against him and his friends Guillaume Farel and Pierre Viret in the 1530s to his debates with the Italian anti-Trinitarians Giorgio Biandrata and Valentino Gentile in the 1550s, the French divine is increasingly conscious of being an heir of the Patristic formulation of the doctrine of the Trinity. But as a minister of the gospel under the authority of the Word of God alone, he was also determined, he said, not to "venture to make any assertion where Scripture is silent."[53] As Calvin read the Scriptures, he saw, as had the Fathers before him, that it clearly sets forth the oneness of the Three—Father, Son and Holy Spirit. At the same time, though, the restraint of scriptural declaration about the relationships within the immanent Trinity required great circumspection in theological reflection on the Godhead.

What needed to be said most clearly in the eyes of Calvin was well summed up by a saying of the Greek Christian author Gregory of Nazianzus (c.330–389), which, Calvin said, gave him vast delight: "I cannot think on the one without quickly being encircled by the splendour of the three; nor can I discern the three without being straightway carried back to the one."[54]

---

53 Commentary on Isaiah 6:2 in *Commentary on the Book of the Prophet Isaiah*, trans. Pringle, 1:203.

54 *Institutes* 1.13.17.

5

Regeneration and faith according to two British Reformed confessions

John Knox and James Ussher

It's not a blind faith will do thee good; the Word of
God works faith in thee; thou hast not a Will to it
born in thee. It is not a flower that grows in thine
own Garden; but is planted by God: John 6:44.
—JAMES USSHER[1]

1 "Redemption by Christ" in *Eighteen Sermons Preached in Oxford 1640* (London: John Rothwell, 1660), 404. This sermon and the others in this book were transcribed by three ministers, Joseph Crabb, William Ball and Thomas Lye. I am indebted to Ian Hugh Clary for this quote. This study was first presented as a paper to the Midwest Founders Conference, St. Louis, Missouri, in 2002. For help on a point of clarification, I wish to thank my brother-in-law, David Livingston-Lowe, of Toronto, Ontario. It has appeared in print as "Regeneration and Faith, according to Two British Confessions,"

In 1582, John Davidson (c.1549–1603), the powerful Scottish Presbyterian preacher known to some in his day as "the thunderer," received
a letter from a Huguenot correspondent in La Rochelle, the bastion of
Calvinism in western France. Soon after, Davidson wrote to another
Calvinist contact, the English Puritan John Field (1545–1588). "It is
no small comfort brother," he told Field, "to brethren of one nation to
understand the state of the brethren in other nations."[2] This seemingly
casual remark is illustrative of the deep sense of solidarity that pre-
vailed among Calvinists in Europe during the sixteenth and seventeenth centuries. One can rightly speak of a Calvinist International,[3]
which, though it received its strength from numerous tributaries
besides the life and work of John Calvin, shared common distinctives
of doctrine, praxis and spirituality.

Now, one of the most important of these distinctives was the conviction, grounded in Scripture and attested to by experience, that entry
into the Christian life is wholly dependent upon God's grace. Consider,
for instance, the *Tetrapolitan Confession*, one of the earliest Reformed
confessions, which was prepared in 1530 by the German Reformers
Martin Bucer, Wolfgang Capito (1478–1541) and Caspar Hedio
(1494/5–1552), and which maintained that "the beginning of all our
righteousness and salvation must proceed from the mercy of the Lord."
In being merciful to fallen men and women, God first "offers the doctrine of truth and his Gospel" through various preachers that he sends
forth to herald the good news about Christ. Due to the fact, though,
that "the natural man receives not the things of the Spirit of God"
(1 Corinthians 2:14), God, the *Tetrapolitan Confession* continues,

> causes a beam of his light to arise at the same time in the dark-
> ness of our heart, so that now we may believe his Gospel preached,

---

The Banner of Truth, 539–540 (August–September 2008): 20–32. Reprinted by
permission.

2   P. Collinson, *Godly People: Essays on English Protestantism and Puritanism* (London:
The Hambledon Press, 1983), 349. My attention was drawn to this remark by Menna
Prestwich, "Introduction: The Changing Face of Calvinism" in Prestwich, ed., *Inter-
national Calvinism 1541–1715* (Oxford: Clarendon Press, 1985), 2.

3   For further exploration of this subject, see especially the various articles in
Prestwich, ed., *International Calvinism.*

being persuaded of the truth thereof by his Spirit from above, and then, relying upon the testimony of this Spirit, may call upon him with filial confidence and say, "Abba, Father," obtaining thereby sure salvation, according to the saying: "Whosoever shall call upon the name of the Lord shall be saved."[4]

Here, regeneration is likened to the illumination of a dark place and its effect is radical indeed. It causes those who are in spiritual darkness to see the truth of the gospel and to believe the gospel as they hear it preached. And vital in this work of regeneration is the Holy Spirit, who enables men and women to call upon the Lord for salvation.

Similarly, at the outset of the Reformation in francophone Geneva, Calvin, possibly with the aid of Guillaume Farel, who we met in the previous chapter and who had first introduced Reformed truth to Geneva, asserted in the 1536 *Geneva Confession* that by God's Spirit

we are regenerated into a new spiritual nature. That is to say that the evil desires of our flesh are mortified by grace, so that they rule us no longer. On the contrary, our will is rendered conformable to God's will, to follow in his way and to seek what is pleasing to him. Therefore we are by him delivered from the servitude of sin, under whose power we were of ourselves held captive, and by this deliverance we are made capable and able to do good works and not otherwise.[5]

In this statement are themes Calvin would return to again and again in the years to come in his voluminous correspondence, sermons and various tracts and treatises. Regeneration is liberation from a slavish dominion, that of "the evil desires of the flesh." Prior to regeneration the human will is in bondage and can make no moves towards doing

---

4   *The Tetrapolitan Confession* III in Arthur C. Cochrane, ed., *Reformed Confessions of the 16th Century* (Philadelphia: Westminster Press, 1966), 58. For the entire confession with an outline of the historical circumstances that prompted it, see Cochrane, ed., *Reformed Confession*, 51–88.

5   *Geneva Confession* 8 in Cochrane, ed., *Reformed Confessions*, 122. For the text of this confession and the historical context in which it was written, see Cochrane, ed., *Reformed Confessions*, 117–126.

what is genuinely pleasing to God. But with regeneration there is "a total transformation and renovation of our wills."[6]

Or look at a later example, from the *Confession of Faith* written by Cyril Lucaris (1572–1638), the Eastern Orthodox Patriarch of Constantinople who embraced the Reformed faith in the second decade of the seventeenth century and was later martyred for his evangelical convictions.[7] In his remarkable *Confession of Faith*, first published in western Europe in Geneva in March 1629, Lucaris declared:

> We believe that free will is dead in the unregenerate, because they can do no good thing, and whatsoever they do is sin; but in the regenerate by the grace of the Holy Spirit the will is excited and in deed worketh but not without the assistance of grace. In order, therefore, that man should be born again and do good, it is necessary that grace should go before; otherwise man is wounded having received as many wounds as that man received who going from Jerusalem down to Jericho fell into the hands of thieves, so that of himself he cannot do anything.[8]

As George Hadjiantoniou notes, Lucaris here "describes with very dark colors the state of the soul before regeneration."[9] He compares the unregenerate to the poor man who was mugged on the Jericho road. After being attacked and left for dead, that man could do nothing to help himself. Similarly, the unregenerate are "wounded" spiritually and "can do no good thing." What they need is the grace given by the Spirit so as to be born again. Then, and only then can they do what is good.

In order to better understand this Reformed consensus on the subject of regeneration and faith, let's focus on two confessional documents. Though both stem from the British Isles, they are written, as we shall

---

6   A.N.S. Lane, "Did Calvin Believe in Freewill?", *Vox Evangelica*, 12 (1981): 81.

7   For the remarkable story of Cyril Lucaris, see George A. Hadjiantoniou, *Protestant Patriarch: the Life of Cyril Lucaris (1572–1638) Patriarch of Constantinople* (Richmond: John Knox Press, 1961). For details about his embrace of what he called "the cause of the Reformers," see Hadjiantoniou, *Protestant Patriarch*, 39–44.

8   *Eastern Confession of the Christian Faith* 14 in Hadjiantoniou, *Protestant Patriarch*, 143.

9   Hadjiantoniou, *Protestant Patriarch*, 97.

see, for somewhat different contexts. But each of them bears witness to the "sense of international solidarity" among sixteenth- and seventeenth-century Calvinists that has been noted above.[10] The first is the *Scottish Confession of Faith* (1560), written by John Knox (*c*.1514–1572) and five others just as the Reformation triumphed in Scotland. It would play a significant role in moulding and shaping the character and religious convictions of numerous Scots in the late sixteenth and early seventeenth centuries. The second text is the *Irish Articles* (1615), adopted by the Church of Ireland at its first convocation and largely drawn up by James Ussher (1581–1656), who was later Archbishop of Armagh. Unlike the *Scottish Confession*, the *Irish Articles* would remain the convictions of but a few in Ireland. If Ussher hoped that this statement of faith would help in the winning of Ireland to the Reformed faith, it was not to be.[11]

THE SCOTTISH CONFESSION OF FAITH (1560)

The *Scottish Confession of Faith* was drawn up in 1560 upon the recommendation of the Scottish Parliament.[12] It followed a political revolt by the Scottish Protestant nobility that secured Scotland for the Reformation and ended what is known the "Auld Alliance" between the Roman Catholic forces of Scotland and France. The *Scottish Confession* is the result of the work of John Knox and five colleagues,[13] who wrote

---

10 The phrase is that of Prestwich, "Introduction" in Prestwich, ed., *International Calvinism*, 5.

11 For a brief overview of the reasons for the failure of the Reformation in Ireland, see Edward Brynn, *The Church of Ireland in the Age of Catholic Emancipation* (New York/ London: Garland Publishing, Inc., 1982), 6–11; Steven G. Ellis, "Ireland" in Hans J. Hillerbrand, ed., *The Oxford Encyclopedia of the Reformation* (New York/Oxford: Oxford University Press, 1996), 2:321–323.

12 For an overview of the context in which this confession was drawn up and its contents, see James Kirk, "Scottish Confession" in Hillerbrand, ed., *Oxford Encyclopedia of the Reformation*, 4:33–36. The version of the confession used in this paper is *The Scottish Confession of Faith* (Dallas: Presbyterian Heritage Publications, 1992).

13 Interestingly enough all of them shared a common first name: John Winram, John Spottiswoode, John Willcock, John Douglas and John Row. On the differences between these men, see Kirk, "Scottish Confession" in Hillerbrand, ed., *Oxford Encyclopedia*, 4:33–34. For a good overview of the life of Knox, see Christopher Catherwood, *Five Leading Reformers* (Tain: Christian Focus, 2000), 161–178. A helpful introduction

the confession within four days of its being commissioned. Approval of it was given by the Scottish Parliament on August 24, 1560, though it would not be formally ratified until 1567. It would remain the doctrinal standard of the Church of Scotland until the *Westminster Standards* were adopted in 1647. The first three editions of the *Scottish Confession* appear to have been in Scots, a cognate language of modern English spoken at the time in much of the Scottish lowlands.[14]

The *Scottish Confession* consists of twenty-five articles which are in broad agreement with the theology of other Reformed confessions of the era. In the words of W. Stanford Reid, the confession "expresses the convictions of men who were thoroughly convinced that the Calvinistic or Reformed doctrines alone are those which represent full-orbed Christianity."[15] Reid points out the significance of this confessional document when he states that it summed up the Reformation's triumph in Scotland, for it "set forth its [ie. the Reformation's] principles for all to receive and follow."[16]

The article that deals with regeneration and faith at length is Article 12, entitled "Faith in the Holy Ghost."

> This our faith, and the assurance of the same, proceeds not from flesh and blood, that is to say, from no natural powers within us, but is the inspiration of the Holy Ghost; whom we confess God, equal with the Father and with his Son, who sanctifies us, and brings us in all verity by his own operation; without whom we

---

to Knox's theology is found in Richard G. Kyle and Dale W. Johnson, *John Knox: An Introduction to His Life and Works* (Eugene: Wipf and Stock, 2009). See also W. Stanford Reid, "John Calvin, John Knox, and the Scottish Reformation" in James E. Bradley and Richard A. Muller, ed., *Church, Word, and Spirit: Historical and Theological Essays in Honour of Geoffrey W. Bromiley* (Grand Rapids: William B. Eerdmans Publ. Co., 1987), 141–151. For a succinct account of the Scottish Reformation, see W. Stanford Reid, "The Triumph of the Reformation in Scotland" in Alan L. Farris, ed., *Reformed and Reforming* (Toronto: Presbyterian Publications, 1960), 19–40.

14 For an edition of the *Confession* in Scots, see *Scots Confession, 1560 [Confessio Scoticana] and Negative Confession, 1581 [Confessio Negativa]*, intro. G.D. Henderson (Edinburgh: Church of Scotland Committee of Publications, 1937).

15 "Triumph of the Reformation in Scotland," 39.

16 "Triumph of the Reformation in Scotland," 40.

John Knox
c.1514–1572

should remain for ever enemies to God, and ignorant of his Son, Christ Jesus. For of nature we are so dead, so blind and so perverse, that neither can we feel when we are pricked, see the light when it shines, nor assent to the will of God when it is revealed, unless the Spirit of the Lord Jesus quicken that which is dead, remove the darkness from our minds, and bow our stubborn hearts to the obedience of his blessed will. And so, as we confess that God the Father created us when we were not; as his Son, our Lord Jesus redeemed us when we were enemies to him; so also do we confess that the Holy Ghost does sanctify and regenerate us, without all respect of any merit proceeding from us, be it before or after our regeneration. To speak this thing yet in more plain words: as we willingly spoil ourselves of all honour and glory of our own creation and redemption, so do we also of our regeneration and sanctification; for of ourselves we are not sufficient to think one good thought; but he who has begun the good work in us, is only he that continues us in the same, to the praise and glory of his undeserved grace.[17]

There are three noteworthy points about this statement that relate to the subject of regeneration and faith. First, Christian faith and the subsequent assurance of that faith, the *Scottish Confession* affirms, do not arise from mere human insight. They are a direct result of the Spirit's supernatural work. As scriptural proof, the compilers of this confession looked to four texts, one from the Gospel of Matthew and three from the farewell discourse in John 14–16.[18] The one from Matthew is Jesus' statement in Matthew 16:17 about Peter's declaration that Jesus is "the Christ, the Son of the living God." This declaration of the truth about Christ is something that God the Father revealed to

---

17 Article 12 (*Scottish Confession of Faith*, 20–21).

18 It should be noted that in the earliest editions of the *Scottish Confession*, references were made simply to book and chapter in Scripture, since versification was not then in general use. For the particular verses upon which this *Confession* is drawing, I have followed the edition of the *Confession* issued by Presbyterian Heritage Publications. For the verses, see also *Confessio fidei Scoticana* in Philip Schaff, ed., *The Creeds of Christendom*, rev. David S. Schaff, 1931 ed. (Reprint, Grand Rapids: Baker Book House, 1983), III, 450–451.

Peter. It was not an insight that a fallible, fallen human being like Peter
could have arrived at on his own. The Johannine texts all relate to Jesus'
teaching about the Holy Spirit's ministry. His ministry is to be one of
teaching (John 14:26), teaching that is particularly centred on the
words and deeds of Christ. And his work among humanity is shaped
by his character as the Spirit of truth (John 15:26) and as such he will
teach what is true, especially about Christ (John 16:13).

Now, according to earlier statements in the *Scottish Confession*,
Christ is "very God and very man, two perfect natures united and
joined in one person."[19] And though he never ceased to be "clean and
innocent" and the "well-beloved and blessed Son of his Father," he was
crucified and "suffered for a season the wrath of his Father, which
sinners had deserved." By his death he made "full satisfaction for the
sins of the people."[20] And since "it was impossible that the dolours[21] of
death should retain in bondage the Author of life," Christ rose from
the dead "for our justification," and so "brought life again to us that
were subject to death and the bondage of the same."[22] Moreover, Christ
is "the only Head of his kirk, our just Lawgiver, our only High priest,
Advocate, and Mediator."[23] Genuine faith, the *Scottish Confession* is
thus arguing in Article 12, is a persuasion about the truth of these vital
matters relating to Christ's person and work—as well other central
matters of the Christian faith that had been laid out in the previous
eleven Articles—a persuasion that is the handiwork of the Spirit.

Second, that the Holy Spirit is well qualified to bring men and
women to such saving faith in Christ is seen in the fact that he is God,
co-equal with the Father and the Son. A classical, biblical Trinitarianism had already been affirmed in the first article of the confession
when it was stated that God is "one in substance, and yet distinct in
three persons: the Father, the Son, and the Holy Ghost."[24] The deity of
the Spirit is important in this matter of regeneration since only One

19 Article 6 (*Scottish Confession of Faith*, 15).
20 Article 9 (*Scottish Confession of Faith*, 17–18).
21 Middle English word, meaning pain or sorrow.
22 Article 10 (*Scottish Confession of Faith*, 18).
23 Article 11 (*Scottish Confession of Faith*, 20).
24 Article 1 (*Scottish Confession of Faith*, 12).

who has invincible power can overcome the insuperable barrier to salvation posed by our fallen human nature, which is a direct result of the Fall of Adam.

The impact that the historical Fall had upon humanity was spelled out in Article 3. There it was stated that this event had caused the "image of God [to be] utterly defaced in man." The result was that all of Adam's progeny became "enemies to God, slaves to Satan and servants to sin." As W. Stanford Reid notes, this forceful statement leaves no room for sinners to save themselves, either by their own works or by anything other fallen creatures can do for them.[25] Fallen humanity thus finds itself in a dreadful state. In Article 12 this state is described as one of spiritual death (Ephesians 2:1; Colossians 2:13), of complete blindness to divine realities (John 9:39; Revelation 3:17) and of utter perversity of will that refuses to heed God (Matthew 17:17; Mark 9:19; Luke 9:41). The sole remedy is the power of the Holy Spirit, who alone can "quicken that which is dead" (Ephesians 2:1; Colossians 2:13; John 6:63), "remove the darkness from our minds" (Micah 7:8) and "bow our stubborn hearts to the obedience of his blessed will" (1 Kings 8:57–58). As the closing words of Article 3 of this confession put it, dead sinners must be

> regenerated from above: which regeneration is wrought by the power of the Holy Ghost, working in the hearts of the elect of God an assured faith in the promise of God, revealed to us in his word; by which faith we apprehend Christ Jesus, with the graces and benefits promised in him.[26]

This radical affirmation of the essential sinfulness of all human activity before regeneration and the exercise of saving faith flies in the face of sixteenth-century Roman Catholic thought. The latter—typified, for example, in the decrees of the Council of Trent (1545–1563)—assumed that the sinfulness of human beings had not so bound their wills that they could not cooperate with God's grace in preparing

25 "Triumph of the Reformation in Scotland," 39.
26 Article 3 (*Scottish Confession of Faith*, 13).

themselves to receive the Spirit's saving grace.[27] The *Scottish Confession* unequivocally rejects the possibility of such collaboration between the sinner and the Spirit. The sinner is utterly dead to God, and nothing he or she does can aid or further the Spirit's quickening work.

Third, the end of this article sounds a further "adversarial note" against Roman Catholicism.[28] Both late mediæval Catholic theology and the promulgations of the Council of Trent essentially constructed a merit theology in which God ultimately gives eternal life as a reward to those who cooperate with his grace and do meritorious deeds.[29] The closing sentences of Article 12, however, underscore the fact that the Spirit's work in regeneration is purely "undeserved grace." Neither anything a sinner does before regeneration, nor anything he or she does after, is to be regarded as deserving of the life that the Spirit of God gives. Just as the Father brought us into being from non-existence as it were, and the Son redeemed us when we were in a state of enmity with God, so the Holy Spirit bestows life on the undeserving, those who possess absolutely nothing to merit his favour. Moreover, from the theological vantage-point of this confession, any talk of human merit not only contradicts the scriptural emphasis of salvation by grace alone, but also robs God of his glory.

THE IRISH ARTICLES (1615)

Due to the fact of English hegemony in Ireland, a Reformed church was established as the state church in that land. But until 1615 this church body, the Church of Ireland, did not have a statement of faith that corresponded, for example, to *The Thirty-nine Articles* (1563) of the Church of England. In 1615, James I called the first convocation of the Church of Ireland to deal specifically with this issue.[30] The result

---

27 Bernard M.G. Reardon, *Religious thought in the Reformation* (London/New York: Longman, 1981), 311; Jan Rohls, *Reformed Confessions: Theology from Zurich to Barmen*, trans. John Hoffmeyer (Louisville: Westminster John Knox Press, 1997), 122–126.

28 Kirk, "Scottish Confession" in Hillerbrand, ed., *Oxford Encyclopedia*, 4:34. For further discussion of the anti-Roman Catholic thrust of the *Scottish Confession*, see G.D. Henderson, "Introduction" to *Scots Confession*, 1560, 15–16.

29 Roger E. Olson, *The Story of Christian Theology: Twenty Centuries of Tradition & Reform* (Downers Grove: InterVarsity Press, 1999), 445–447.

30 Norman Sykes, "James Ussher as Churchman," *Theology*, 60 (1957): 57.

was the *Irish Articles*, which were chiefly drawn up by James Ussher, who, at the time, was Vice-Chancellor of Trinity College, Dublin, and whom Samuel Johnson (1709–1784) called "the great luminary of the Irish Church."[31] Ussher was renowned as the leading British biblical and patristic scholar of his day and was also a staunch defender of Episcopal church government. He was also widely respected for being staunchly Calvinistic to the core and for his winsome, gentle character.[32]

As D.F. Kelly observes, the *Irish Articles* are "considerably more Calvinistic" than the *Thirty-nine Articles*.[33] Arranged under nineteen headings, the 104 articles strongly set forth, among other things, God's sovereignty in predestination—"God hath predestinated some unto

31 For this description, see James Boswell, *The Life of Samuel Johnson L.L.D.* (New York: The Modern Library, Inc., n.d.), 384. For the life and labours of Ussher, see especially James Anderson Carr, *The Life and Times of Archbishop Ussher*, 1895 ed. (Reprint, Green Forest, Alabama: Master Books, 2006); R. Buick Knox, *James Ussher, Archbishop of Armagh* (Cardiff: University of Wales Press, 1967); and Crawford Gribben, *The Irish Puritans: James Ussher and the Reformation of the Church* (Darlington: Evangelical Press, 2003).

For shorter overviews of his life and ministry, the standard is now Alan Ford, "Ussher, James" in H.C.G. Matthew and Brian Harrison, ed., *Oxford Dictionary of National Biography* (Oxford: Oxford University Press, 2004), 56:6–14. See also, though, Philip Styles, "James Ussher and His Times," *Hermathena*, 88 (November 1956): 12–33; Alfonso Ropero, "James Ussher—A Protestant Controversialist," *The Banner of Truth*, 351 (December 1992): 9–11; William S. Barker, *Puritan Profiles: 54 Influential Puritans at the Time When the Westminster Confession of Faith Was Written* (Tain: Christian Focus/Mentor, 1996), 44–47; R.K. Bishop, "Ussher, James" in Walter A. Elwell, ed., *Evangelical Dictionary of Theology*, 2nd ed. (Grand Rapids: Baker Book House/Carlisle: Paternoster Press, 2001), 1234; and Juan José Pérez-Camacho, "Ussher, James" in Brian Lalor, ed., *The Encyclopedia of Ireland* (New Haven/London: Yale University Press, 2003), 1105.

An edition of Ussher's works was published in the nineteenth century by C.R. Elrington and J.H. Todd, ed., *The Whole Works of the Most Rev. James Ussher* (Dublin: Hodges & Smith/London: Whittaker & Co, 1847–1864), 17 vols.

Finally, see the very useful website "The Ussher Project" (http://www.tcd.ie/history/Ussher/home.php; accessed May 10, 2011), which is seeking to produce a scholarly three-volume edition of the correspondence of Ussher. It contains a life of Ussher and an extensive bibliography of primary and secondary sources.

32 Bishop, "Ussher, James" in Elwell, ed., *Evangelical Dictionary of Theology*, 1234.

33 "Irish Articles" in Elwell, ed., *Evangelical Dictionary of Theology*, 617.

James Ussher
1581–1656

Credit: Portrait circa 1647. © Hulton Archive/Getty Images.

life, and reprobated some unto death"[34]—the typical Puritan view of the Lord's day[35] and that the pope is the Antichrist.[36] What is amazing, given Ussher's convictions about episcopacy, is that there is not a word about church government in the document.

The key articles that relate to regeneration and its fruit are Articles 32–33 under the heading "Of the communicating of the grace of Christ."

> 32. None can come unto Christ unless it be given unto him, and unless the Father draw him. And all men are not so drawn by the Father that they may come unto the Son. Neither is there such a sufficient measure of grace vouchsafed unto every man whereby he is enabled to come unto everlasting life.
>
> 33. All God's elect are in their time inseparably united unto Christ by the effectual and vital influence of the Holy Ghost, derived from him as from the head unto every true member of his mystical body. And being thus made one with Christ, they are truly regenerated and made partakers of him and all his benefits.[37]

The wording of the first of these articles has been taken almost verbatim from the eighth and ninth of the *Lambeth Articles*, which had been drawn up in 1595 by a committee under the chairmanship of John Whitgift (c.1530–1604), the Archbishop of Canterbury who is usually remembered for his strong antipathy to Puritanism. These nine articles had powerfully affirmed a "predestinarian theology of grace" and had been drawn up in response to a controversy at the University of Cambridge over Calvinism, a forerunner of the later Arminian controversy.[38]

---

34 *Irish Articles of Religion* 12, Schaff, ed., *Creeds of Christendom*, III, 528.

35 *Irish Articles of Religion* 56, Schaff, ed., *Creeds of Christendom*, III, 536.

36 *Irish Articles of Religion* 80, Schaff, ed., *Creeds of Christendom*, III, 540.

37 Schaff, ed., *Creeds of Christendom*, III, 532.

38 Dewey D. Wallace, Jr., *Puritans and Predestination: Grace in English Protestant Theology, 1525–1695* (Chapel Hill: University of North Carolina Press, 1982), 66–67. For the text of the Articles and a discussion of them, see H.C. Porter, *Reformation and Reaction in Tudor Cambridge*, 1958 ed. (Reprint, Hamden: Archon Books, 1972), 364–371.

Article 32 of the *Irish Articles* begins with a clear allusion to Jesus' teaching in John 6:44 that for a person to come to Christ he or she must be drawn to the Saviour by God the Father. Since not all human beings come to Christ, it must then be the case that not all of them receive grace to do so. Those who do receive such grace are described by Article 33 as "God's elect." An earlier article, Article 15, had denominated such individuals as those who are "predestinated unto life."[39] All of the elect or predestined do indeed in due time receive sufficient grace to bring them to Christ.[40] The *Irish Articles* maintain that this grace is given to them by the "effectual and vital" power of the Spirit, who unites them to Christ and so brings them into a union that entails regeneration.[41]

Regeneration here is particularly viewed as part of God's effectual calling of individuals. Although a later article dealing with justification attacks the whole Roman Catholic notion of merit,[42] that anti-Catholic note is not at all evident in the treatment of regeneration in Article 12. Rather, regeneration is presented as part of the *ordo salutis*, and explicitly linked to predestination and effectual calling.

This perspective on regeneration clearly reflects Ussher's own tendency to view salvation as a whole through a predestinarian lens. For example, in a sermon entitled *The True Intent and Extent of Christ's Death and Satisfaction upon the Cross*, which was published in 1617, the Irish theologian declared:

[T]he Lamb of God, offering himself a sacrifice for the sins of the whole world, intended by giving sufficient satisfaction to God's

---

39 Schaff, ed., *Creeds of Christendom*, III, 529.

40 Cp. also *Irish Articles of Religion* 15, Schaff, ed., *Creeds of Christendom*, III, 529: "Such as are predestinated unto life be called according unto God's purpose (his Spirit working in due season) and through grace they obey the calling."

41 For the background of the thinking at this point, see Wallace, *Puritans and Predestination*, 49–50.

42 *Irish Articles of Religion* 36, Schaff, ed., *Creeds of Christendom*, III, 533, where it states that "we must renounce the merit of all our said virtues, of faith, hope, charity, and all our other virtues and good deeds which we either have done, shall do, or can do, as things that be far too weak and imperfect and insufficient to deserve remission of our sins and our justification, and therefore we must trust only in God's mercy and the merits of his most dearly beloved Son, our only Redeemer, Saviour, and Justifier, Jesus Christ."

justice, to make the nature of man which he assumed a fit subject for mercy, and to prepare a medicine for the sins of the whole world, which should be denied to none that intended to take the benefit of it; howsoever he intended not by applying this all-sufficient remedy unto every person in particular to make it effectual unto the salvation of all, or to procure thereby the actual pardon for the sins of the whole world.[43]

The treatment of regeneration in Article 12 also reflects, however, the beginning of what would be a massive controversy within the international Calvinist community over the teaching of Jacob Arminius (1560–1609), a professor at Leiden. Arminius and his followers maintained, among other things, that predestination was simply God's advance knowledge of who would actually respond to the gospel, that Christ's death obtained for every human being the possibility of salvation, and that the Holy Spirit's regenerating grace was not necessarily irresistible.[44]

Ussher could not have been oblivious to the growing storm over Arminianism. The *Irish Articles* are unequivocal in their rejection of any hint of this theological position.[45] Consider Article 14 in this regard, where the *Irish Articles* draw upon the second of the *Lambeth Articles* to state that:

The cause moving God to predestinate unto life is not the fore-seeing of faith, or perseverance, or good works, or of any thing which is in the person predestinated, but only the good pleasure of God himself. For all things being ordained for the manifestation of his glory, and his glory being to appear both in the works of his mercy and of his justice, it seemed good to his heavenly wisdom to choose out a certain number towards whom he would

---

43 Cited Sykes, Sykes, "James Ussher as Churchman," 58–59.

44 Peter Toon, *Born Again: A Biblical and Theological Study of Regeneration* (Grand Rapids: Baker Book House, 1987), 118–120. See the very helpful study of Arminianism by Alan P.F. Sell, *The Great Debate: Calvinism, Arminianism and Salvation,* 1982 ed. (Reprint, Eugene: Wipf & Stock, 1998), 5–14.

45 Sell, *Great Debate,* 26–27.

extend his undeserved mercy, leaving the rest to be spectacles of his justice.[46]

CONCLUDING THOUGHTS

The treatment of regeneration in the *Scottish Confession* seeks to dismantle every inkling of the merit theology of Roman Catholicism, while the need to respond to a new foe, Arminianism, seems to have shaped the way in which the *Irish Articles* deal with regeneration and explicitly embed it in the *ordo salutis*. These differences aside, they reveal two commonalities to all Reformed thought in this period: a desire to highlight that salvation is due to pure grace alone and that thinking anything less is injurious to the great end of human existence—the glorifying of God alone.

---

46 Schaff, ed., *Creeds of Christendom*, III, 529.

6

A pioneer of Puritan soul care
Richard Greenham

We look not for the Spirit in our fantasy, but for the
Spirit which worketh by the Word. —RICHARD GREENHAM

Although the Reformation had come to England during the reign of
Henry VIII (r.1509–1547), it was not until the reign of his son Edward
VI and that of his daughter Elizabeth I that it got a firm footing. In fact,
after Elizabeth I ascended the throne there was no doubt that England
was firmly in the Protestant orbit. The question that arose, though,
was to what extent the Elizabethan church would be reformed. It soon
became clear that Elizabeth was content with a church that was "Calvinistic in theology, [but] Erastian in Church order and government
[ie. the state was ascendant over the church in these areas], and
largely mediæval in liturgy."[1] In response to this ecclesiastical "settledness" there arose the Puritan movement in the early 1560s that sought

---

1   Robert C. Walton, *The Gathered Community* (London: Carey Press, 1946), 59.

to reform the Elizabethan church after the model of the churches in Protestant Switzerland, especially those in Geneva and Zürich. The Puritan work of reformation focused on three main institutions: the university, the parish church and the family.

First, the biblical education of pastors at the university—of the two universities, Oxford and Cambridge, Cambridge University especially became the nursery of Puritan ministers—was vital if reformation was to be deep and long-lasting. Then, there was the hard work of reforming the local church and the family. When it comes to these latter institutions, Richard Greenham (c.1540/45–1594) has been rightly identified as the first of a great line of English Puritan pastors, the pioneer of Puritan pastoral care.[2] Some years after his death, he was reckoned to be among the three or four most important figures of the Elizabethan church, renowned for his skill as spiritual guide. And, yet, as Eric Josef Carlson has noted, "for centuries he has almost vanished from the historical record, thanks to his decision to labor in the relatively obscure rural Cambridgeshire parish of Dry Drayton."[3] Apart from a 1920 doctoral dissertation, there was no modern major study of his life and work until 1998. That year two studies appeared, to both of which I am deeply indebted for the sketch of his life and legacy that follows: Kenneth L. Parker and Eric J. Carlson, 'Practical Divinity': The Works and Life of Revd Richard Greenham[4] and John H. Primus, Richard Greenham: Portrait of an Elizabethan Pastor.[5]

---

2   O.R. Johnston, "Richard Greenham and the Trials of a Christian" in D. Martyn Lloyd-Jones, ed., Puritan Papers. Volume 1, 1956–1959 (Phillipsburg: Presbyterian and Reformed Publishing Co., 2000), 71. For the dates of Greenham, see Stanley Jebb, "Richard Greenham and the Counselling of Troubled Souls" in Puritans and Spiritual Life. Papers read at the 2001 Westminster Conference (London: The Westminster Conference, 2001), 82.

3   Eric Josef Carlson, "Book Reviews: Richard Greenham: Portrait of an Elizabethan Pastor. John H. Primus", The Sixteenth Century Journal, 30, no.1 (Spring, 1999): 239–240; Kenneth L. Parker and Eric J. Calrson, 'Practical Divinity': The Works and Life of Revd Richard Greenham (Aldershot: Ashgate, 1998), 5.

4   Parker and Carlson, 'Practical Divinity.'

5   John H. Primus, Richard Greenham: Portrait of an Elizabethan Pastor (Macon: Mercer University Press, 1998).

MINISTER OF DRY DRAYTON

Prior to his matriculation at Pembroke Hall at Cambridge University in 1559 we have no accurate knowledge of his birthplace and early years.[6] From 1559 to 1570, Greenham's home was Cambridge. These were the early halcyon days of the reign of Elizabeth I, when all Protestants were thrilled to have a Protestant queen. Greenham graduated in 1563–1564, by which time the term "Puritan" had come into existence as a term denoting those radical Protestants who were conscious that they had been saved by God through no merits of their own but whose salvation was ultimately a matter of his electing mercy, which doctrinal conviction we have looked at in detail in the previous chapter. They had been saved so as to live lives of visible piety within churches that were to be patterned after the New Testament. And part of the Puritan hope was that collectively their visible piety would refashion their society into a model Christian community.[7] Greenham spent most of his pastoral career, from 1570 to 1590, in the small parish of St. Peter and St. Paul, Dry Drayton, Cambridgeshire, a few miles north of Cambridge, where he came after studying at Cambridge. It was a small parish of only about 150 people.[8]

John Primus sees Greenham as representative of a moderate form of Puritanism that was typical of the Puritan movement in the Elizabethan era. This was a form of Puritanism that was loyal both to the English crown and to the state-established Church of England. Primus is rightly convinced that describing any Puritan as a "moderate" is an oxymoron since the Puritans were passionately committed to a radical form of Christianity. He therefore suggests that the term "cooperative Puritanism" would be a more appropriate term for men like Greenham, since Greenham's type of Puritanism cooperated with the established religious and political order. For example, he had no problems with the giving of the marriage ring in the marriage ceremony, a ritual that most Puritan ministers refused to sanction, claiming that it had pagan origins in England's Anglo-Saxon past.[9] Yet, he was clearly

---

6   Primus, *Richard Greenham*, 12–13.

7   John Spurr, *English Puritanism 1603–1689* (London: Macmillan, 1998), 5.

8   Carlson, "Book Reviews: *Richard Greenham*", 240.

9   Parker and Carlson, '*Practical Divinity*,' 80.

Puritan in his refusal to wear what were the designated vestments for leading worship.[10]

A PREACHING MINISTRY

In a letter to his bishop, Greenham described his ministry as "preaching Christ crucified unto myself and Country people." On another occasion Greenham summed up pastoral ministry thus: it is "none other thing, but to preach the word of God sincerely, and purely with a care of the glory of God, and a desire of the salvation of our brethren: & secondly a reverent administration of the sacraments."[11] And again, Greenham could state: "such horrible disorder is there, where God's Word is not truly preached."[12] In this high estimation of preaching as the central role of pastoral ministry, Greenham was a typical Puritan and a typical child of the Reformation.

Now, it is noteworthy that, in the Elizabethan Age, it was not just the Puritans who were concerned about preaching—their opponents within the English Church were also convinced of its importance. As Winthrop Hudson notes, the "century following Elizabeth's accession [in 1559] was one of the great ages of the pulpit."[13] Part of the reason for this was the fact that newspapers and other forms of information media had yet to make their appearance and a sermon could be a major source of information and political comment. More importantly, the Elizabethan church had inherited the problem from the mediæval church of widespread ignorance among the people—in Dry Drayton, female illiteracy was virtually one hundred per cent, while male illiteracy was seventy per cent[14]—and also among the clergy. Among the latter "many knew little or no Latin and less Scripture—indeed, some could barely read the English services of the new Prayer Book." All parties within the Church of England, therefore, recognized the need for theological education via the pulpit. Thus, George Herbert (1593–

---

10 Jebb, "Richard Greenham and the Counselling of Troubled Souls", 83.

11 Cited Parker and Carlson, 'Practical Divinity,' 59.

12 Cited Jebb, "Richard Greenham and the Counselling of Troubled Souls," 85.

13 Winthrop Hudson, "The Ministry in the Puritan Age" in H. Richard Niebuhr and Daniel D. Williams, ed., The Ministry in Historical Perspectives (New York: Harper & Brothers, 1956), 185.

14 Primus, Richard Greenham, 32.

1633), the Anglican poet and pastor, was insistent that the "country parson" should preach constantly—"the pulpit is his joy and throne."[15] But it was especially among the Puritans that the importance of the pulpit and preaching was emphasized. As Irvonwy Morgan puts it: "the essential thing in understanding the Puritans is that they were preachers before they were anything else."[16] For the Puritans, the pulpit was a place of fire and light, a place that stirred up hearts to follow after Christ, a place that brought sight to the blind and further enlightenment to believers.

Nicholas Bownde, Greenham's stepson, who was a Suffolk Puritan minister and who published the first major Puritan exposition of Sunday as the Sabbath, *A True Doctrine of the Sabbath* (1595), could declare that preaching the Word of God is "the greatest part of God's service."[17] Again, George Downame (1560–1634), who heard Greenham preach in Cambridge, called preaching "the chief worke of the Ministerie."[18] One of the men whom Greenham mentored, Arthur Hildersham (1563–1632), the son of zealous Roman Catholics who had hoped that their son would become a Roman Catholic priest and who was disinherited after his conversion, could state: "Preaching...is the chief work that we are called of God to exercise ourselves in."[19]

Due to the fact that numerous demands on his time gave him little free time during the day, Greenham would rise at four every day to study and prepare his sermons. During the week he preached a sermon on Monday, Tuesday, Wednesday and Friday just after dawn so that his parishioners might attend before they went to work. After preaching he would go back to study in the morning, and then in the afternoon he visited the sick or went out into the fields to speak with his parishioners as they were working.[20] His zeal for the souls of his parishioners

---

15 Hudson, "Ministry in the Puritan Age," 186.

16 Cited John H. Primus, *Holy Time: Moderate Puritanism and the Sabbath* (Macon: Mercer University Press, 1989), 170.

17 Cited Primus, *Holy Time*, 174.

18 Cited Parker and Carlson, 'Practical Divinity,' 61.

19 Cited Peter Lewis, *The Genius of Puritanism*, 2nd ed. (Haywards Heath: Carey Press, 1979), 35. On Hildersham's background and his relationship to Greenham, see Parker and Carlson, 'Practical Divinity,' 32, 46, 95. See also later in this chapter.

20 Parker and Carlson, 'Practical Divinity,' 63.

led him to trudge through the clay furrows of the fields, so as to speak to the men of his flock as they worked. He preached twice on Sundays. And on Thursday morning he catechized the children of the parish, which he also did each Sunday evening.

According to Henry Holland (d.1603), who was the seventeenth-century editor of Greenham's collected works, and who wrote a short memoir of Greenham to accompany his edition of his works, Greenham preached with such energy that "his shirt would usually be as wet with sweating, as if it had been drenched in water."[21] Before he went into the pulpit, though, he often experienced what he regarded as Satanic attacks: "very sharp and trembling fears in the flesh" would assail him.[22]

On one occasion as Greenham was preaching, a woman in the congregation suddenly burst into loud weeping and crying out she was a damned soul. Greenham had to stop preaching and go down to console her. "Woman," he said to her, "didst thou not come into this place to hear of thy sins and the forgiveness of them in Christ: be of good comfort, and as thou seest thy sins so shalt thou hear pardon" of them.[23] Such an immediate and visible impact of the Word, though, does not appear to have been the norm. But, in time, Greenham did become well-known as a powerful preacher and was invited to regularly preach in Cambridge, at Great St. Mary's, as well as elsewhere.

A COUNSELLING MINISTRY

Greenham was well known and appreciated as a gospel preacher, but it was as a pastoral counsellor that he excelled. John Primus has argued persuasively that in this area Greenham was "an ecclesiastical titan who used his extraordinary gifts to make enormous contributions to God's church and kingdom."[24] For Greenham also, to fulfill his ministry as a preacher meant pastoral visitation. This enabled him to engage in what he called "Christian conferring," which he considered a very helpful means of grace alongside listening to the preached Word and

---

21 Cited Parker and Carlson, 'Practical Divinity,' 62.
22 Cited Parker and Carlson, 'Practical Divinity,' 62.
23 Cited Parker and Carlson, 'Practical Divinity,' 62.
24 Richard Greenham, 7.

reading the Bible for oneself [25]—recall, though, the high percentage of illiteracy in the congregation would hinder the latter. According to Henry Holland, Greenham

> having great Experience and an excellent Faculty to relieve and comfort distressed Consciences, he was sought to, far and near, by such as groaned under spiritual Afflictions and temptations... the fame of this spiritual Physician so spread abroad that he was sent for to very many, and the Lord was pleased so far to bless his labours that by his knowledge and experience many were restored to joy and comfort.

Alongside this ministry of counselling was that of catechizing, which Greenham regarded as an essential corollary for successful preaching. He catechized Sunday afternoons and then also on mid-Thursday afternoons.[26] A typical catechism of that era included four elements: the decalogue, the Apostles' Creed, the Lord's Prayer and the sacraments. Greenham, in fact, drew up his own catechism. The extant version of it only contains the first two items of a typical Elizabethan catechism. This is probably due to the fact that the copies we have of his catechism are incomplete,[27] even though the copies we do have contain over 300 questions and short answers.[28]

Greenham's friends hoped he would write a book on the art of counselling, but he never did. He did pass on a great deal of his wisdom to others by word of mouth. In their volume on Greenham, Parker and Carlson have published a copy of Greenham's sayings that were drawn up after his death.[29] These pithy sayings reveal Greenham to be a man of rare wisdom. Here are three good examples of his wisdom:

Many are barren in grace because they are barren in prayer.[30]

---

25 Parker and Carlson, 'Practical Divinity,' 64–65.
26 Parker and Carlson, 'Practical Divinity,' 69.
27 Parker and Carlson, 'Practical Divinity,' 69, 70.
28 For some examples, see Parker and Carlson, 'Practical Divinity,' 295–296.
29 'Practical Divinity,' 127–259.
30 'Practical Divinity,' 232.

Concerning recreations, he could not away that they should be
to pass away the time seeing the Holy Ghost did will us to redeem
to the time.[31]

Where the Scripture hath not a mouth, we ought not to have ears.[32]

Yet, he was also a man of his own time. For instance, when he was
asked "what he thought of fairies, he answered he thought they
were spirits."[33]

MENTORING PASTORS

Yet, for all his godliness, insight, evangelical message and hard work,
his ministry was virtually fruitless. Others outside his parish were
blessed through him, but not his own people. A little rhyme that
expressed this fact made the circle among the Puritans: "Greenham
had pastures green, but flocks full lean."[34] "I perceive no good wrought
by my ministry on any but one family" was what, according to Holland,
he said to his successor.

In rural England in Greenham's day, there was much fallow ground
to be broken up. It was a time for sowing, and the time for reaping
was still in the future. Part of the breaking up of the fallow ground
involved the training of ministers. It is noteworthy that there was no
provision at that time of the practical training of ministers. Greenham recommended and actually was vitally involved in the mentoring
of various men.[35] For example, among key Puritan leaders that he
trained and mentored were Arthur Hildersham, Henry Smith
(c.1560–1591) and Joseph Hall (1574–1656). In this way, Parker and
Carlson note, "literally thousands of English lay people were, by the
1620s, in some sense the flock of Richard Greenham."[36]

---

31 'Practical Divinity,' 181–182.
32 Primus, Richard Greenham, 90.
33 'Practical Divinity,' 159.
34 Cited Primus, Richard Greenham, 51.
35 Jebb, "Richard Greenham and the Counselling of Troubled Souls," 83–84.
36 'Practical Divinity,' 21–22.

PREACHING ON THE HOLY SPIRIT

In the twentieth century, a good number of Pentecostals thought, wrongly as church history would have it, that they were the first movement since the apostolic era to really have made much of the Spirit. In fact, that honour probably belongs to the Puritans, if we are thinking of the work of the Holy Spirit. Listen to Richard Lovelace:

> Among the Reformers, John Calvin has been called the theologian of the Holy Spirit because his doctrinal work so carefully honors the sovereign agency of the Spirit in regeneration and sanctification. This emphasis continued in the Reformed tradition, for the English Puritans (particularly John Owen and Richard Sibbes) have given us the most profound and extensive biblical-theological studies of the ministry of the Holy Spirit which exist in any language.[37]

Or listen to the Presbyterian theologian Benjamin B. Warfield in his "Introductory Note" to Abraham Kuyper's *The Work of the Holy Spirit*:

> ...the developed doctrine of the work of the Holy Spirit is an exclusively Reformation doctrine, and more particularly a Reformed doctrine, and more particularly still a Puritan doctrine... Puritan thought was almost entirely occupied with loving study of the work of the Holy Ghost, and found its highest expressions in dogmatico-practical expositions of the several aspects of it.[38]

After the apostolic era, it took considerable time and thought to unpack all of the insights of the New Testament with regard to the

---

37 Richard Lovelace, *Dynamics of Spiritual Life. An Evangelical Theology of Renewal* (Downers Grove: Inter-Varsity Press, 1979), 120. See also Richard B. Gaffin, "The Holy Spirit," *The Westminster Theological Journal*, 43 (1980): 61, and the detailed discussion by Garth B. Wilson, "Doctrine of the Holy Spirit in the Reformed Tradition: A Critical Overview," in George Vandervelde, ed., *The Holy Spirit: Renewing and Empowering Presence* (Winfield: Wood Lake Books, 1989), 57–62.

38 Benjamin B. Warfield in his "Introductory Note" to Abraham Kuyper, *The Work of the Holy Spirit*, trans. Henri de Vries, 1900 ed. (Reprint, Grand Rapids: William B. Eerdmans Publ. Co., 1956), xxxiii, xxviii.

person and work of the Holy Spirit. Indeed, the main pneumatological achievement from the period of the New Testament down to the fourth century was focused on the clear recognition and defence of the full deity and personality of the Spirit. This recognition is well seen in the creedal statement of the Council of Constantinople in A.D. 381: "[We believe] in the Holy Spirit, the Lord and Giver of Life, who proceeds from the Father, who with the Father and Son is together worshipped and glorified, who spoke through the prophets." The Puritan emphasis on the Spirit was built on this ontological foundation of the Spirit's deity.

Greenham is then a typical Puritan when it comes to his having a keen pneumatological focus. In a sermon entitled "Of the Sending of the Holy Ghost," he states, for instance: "Above all gifts…in the world this is the gift of gifts, the Spirit of God…This is the top, this is the head, this is the height, this is the depth of all good things even the Spirit."[39] The reason why this is so, Greenham goes on to delineate, is because of the vital necessity of the Spirit's work in our lives for salvation, sanctification, worship, and perseverance.[40] Then, given the Word-centred nature of his Puritan piety, which we have looked at above, Greenham emphasizes the co-ordinate activity of the Spirit and the Word:

> without the Spirit, the Word is as the bright Sun to a blind man… True it is, the Sun is bright, but what is that a blind man? True it is the Word is glorious, but what is that a man without the Spirit of God?

But, Greenham continued,

> we must try the spirits by the word, and we shall then know we have received the Spirit of God…we cannot profit by the word, but by God his spirit: we look not for the Spirit in our fantasy, but for the Spirit which worketh by the word.[41]

---

39 *The Workes of the Reverend and Faithfull Servant of Jesus Christ M. Richard Greenham* (London: William Welby, 1612), 222.

40 *Workes*, 222–223.

41 *Workes*, 223–224.

FINAL DAYS

In 1590 Greenham moved to London for reasons now unknown. He left Dry Drayton in the charge of a Richard Warfield (1558–1620), whom he told: "Mr. Warfield, God bless you, and send you more fruit for your labours than I have had: for I perceive no good wrought by my ministry on any but one family."[42] Of his ministry in the capital of England we know next to nothing, though we do know he later regretted the move to the city.

It is a good thing that God sometimes keeps hidden from his children much of the good they do in this world so that their joy in the world to come might be great and full of glory. We trust Richard Greenham found it so when he left this world of his discipleship in April 1594.

---

42 Cited Primus, *Richard Greenham*, 201.

7

"Zeal to promote the common good"

The story of the King James Bible

Translation it is that openeth the window, to let in the light; that breaketh the shell, that we may eat the kernel; that putteth aside the curtain, that we may look into the most holy place; that removeth the cover of the well, that we may come by the water...
—MILES SMITH[1]

1   "Preface to the Authorised (King James) Version, 1611," par. 5, Gerald Bray, *Translating the Bible from William Tyndale to King James* (London: The Latimer Trust, 2010), 211–212. This chapter was originally given as one of two lectures in the Staley Distinguished Scholar Lecture Series at Charleston Southern University, Charleston, South Carolina, March 8, 2011. It first appeared in print in *The Banner of Truth*, 573 (June 2011) and 574 (July 2011). Reprinted by permission.

The sixteenth century was one of the great eras of English Bible translation. Between 1526, when William Tyndale's superlative rendition
of the New Testament was printed, and 1611, when the King James
Bible (KJB), or Authorized Bible, appeared, no less than ten English-
language Bible versions were published.[2] The translators of the KJB
were quite conscious of their deep indebtedness to this beehive of
translation activity that preceded their work. As they noted in the
"Preface" of the KJB, drawn up by the Puritan Miles Smith (1554–1624),
who had been among those responsible for the translation of the Old
Testament prophets and who had also taken part in the final revision
of the entirety of the Old Testament, they had not sought to "make a
new translation." Rather, it had been their "endeavour" or "mark" to
"make a good one better, or out of many good ones, one principal good
one."[3] And of those many good versions that preceded the KJB, two
especially deserve mention in any sketch of the history of the KJB:
Tyndale's New Testament and the Geneva Bible. We have already looked
at the Tyndale New Testament in chapter 2, and so need not repeat the
details surrounding that translation here. Suffice it to say that Tyndale's
work was so good, it formed the core of the KJB New Testament.

THE GENEVA BIBLE

During the Marian reign of terror,[4] about a thousand English and Scottish Protestants fled to the European continent and found places of

2   The major ones were, in chronological order, the Bible of Miles Coverdale (1535),
"Matthew's Bible" (1537), the Great Bible (1539), the Geneva Bible (1560), the Bishops'
Bible (1568) and the Roman Catholic Douai-Rheims Bible (1582/1610). For details,
see David Daniell, *The Bible in English: Its History and Influence* (New Haven/London:
Yale University Press, 2003). For an older, but still very useful, study of these various
versions, see F.F. Bruce, *History of the Bible in English: From the earliest versions*, 3rd ed.
(New York: Oxford University Press, 1978).

3   "Preface to the Authorised (King James) Version, 1611," par. 13, Bray, *Translating
the Bible*, 228. On Smith, see Edward Irving Carlyle "Smith, Miles", *The Compact Edition
of the Dictionary of National Biography* (London: Oxford University Press, 1975), II,
1948; Gustavus S. Paine, *The Men Behind the King James Version*, 1959 ed. (Reprint,
Grand Rapids: Baker Book House, 1977), *passim*; John Tiller, "In the Steps of William
Tyndale: Miles Smith as Bible Translator", paper given at Gloucester Cathedral,
October 6, 1998; http://www.tyndale.org/TSJ/11/tiller.html; accessed May 11, 2011.

4   See chapter 3.

refuge in Reformed locales like Zürich and Geneva. At this time, Geneva was a major centre of biblical scholarship, with more than thirty publishing houses. In the 1550s alone, these publishers printed new editions of both the Hebrew and Greek Scriptures, supervised at least eight printings of the French Bible and translations of the Scriptures into Italian and Spanish.[5] It is not at all surprising that, in such a climate, the English and Scottish exiles began to plan a new translation of the Bible in 1556 that would eventually be published four years later and that would come to be known as the Geneva Bible. Like all of the English Bibles of this era, except for that of Tyndale, it was the joint product of a group of scholars.

The main translator and editor appears to have been William Whittingham (c.1524–1579), a fellow of All Souls College, Oxford, who was one of the most competent Greek linguists of the day and also fluent in both French and German.[6] Among the sources that Whittingham used was the 1553 edition of the French Bible of Pierre Olivétain (1506–1538), whose New Testament had been corrected by Olivétain's cousin, the great Reformer John Calvin.[7] It is not clear whether Whittingham was responsible for the translation of the Old Testament. What is certain, according to David Daniell, is that the Geneva Bible's Old Testament has a "wonderful richness" and "Britain was truly blessed in the men who made it."[8]

Along with its superb translation of the Old and New Testaments, the Geneva Bible contained a running commentary on the whole Bible in the form of marginal notes, what Patrick Collinson has called a

---

5   Daniell, *Bible in English*, 292–293; Lloyd E. Berry, "Introduction to the Facsimile Edition" in *The Geneva Bible. A facsimile of the 1560 edition* (Madison/London: The University of Wisconsin Press, 1969), 7.

6   Berry, "Introduction to the Facsimile Edition," 8. For an excellent discussion of Whittingham as an editor, see Basil Hall, "The Genevan Version of the English Bible: Its Aims and Achievements" in W.P. Stephens, ed., *The Bible, the Reformation and the Church: Essays in Honour of James Atkinson* (Sheffield: Sheffield Academic Press, 1995), 127–137. On the Geneva Bible, see Daniell, *Bible in English*, 275–319

7   Hall, "Genevan Version of the English Bible" in Stephens, ed., *Bible, the Reformation and the Church*, 140–143. Whittingham was related to Calvin through marriage to his wife's sister, Katherine.

8   Daniell, *Bible in English*, 315.

"portable library of divinity."[9] As shall be seen, some of these marginal notes would infuriate King James I and bias him against this version. The majority of the notes contain helpful explanations of the text. Occasionally there is exhortation and application. For example, with regard to Genesis 24:58 ("And they called Rebekah and said unto her, Wilt thou go with this man?"), the marginal note commented: "This sheweth that parents have not authoritie to marry their children without consent of the parties." Contrary to an impression transmitted among some historians of the English Bible,[10] no more than ten of the original marginal notes, outside of the Book of Revelation, were barbed attacks on other religious perspectives of that era, notably that of the Roman Catholic Church. The marginal notes to the book of Revelation, however, do contain a significant amount of apocalyptic speculation some of which explicitly targets the Roman Church and the papacy.[11] For example, the sternest marginal note in this regard is an explanation of the judgement of painful sores in Revelation 16:2. The note likens this judgement to that of the sixth plague of Egypt and that which "reigneth commonly among canons, monks, friars, nuns, priests, and such filthy vermin which bear the mark of the beast." This is strong stuff, but, as Daniell comments, its tone is not the norm even among the apocalyptic notes on Revelation.[12]

---

9   Patrick Collinson, *The Elizabethan Puritan Movement*, 1967 ed.(Reprint, New York: Methuen & Co., 1982), 365.

10   See, for example, Milton P. Brown, *To Hear the Word. Invitation to Serious Study of the Bible* (Macon: Mercer University Press, 1987), 126: "with the Geneva Bible marginal notes became a vehicle of Protestant propaganda"; Adam Nicolson, *God's Secretaries: The Making of the King James Bible* (New York: HarperCollins, 2003), 249, where mention is made of the Geneva Bible's "highly contentious notes"; and Derek Wilson, *The People's Bible: The Remarkable History of the King James Version* (Oxford: Lion Hudson, 2010), 66: "The notes made the book the most effective piece of propaganda the Calvinist party ever produced."

11   Hall, "Genevan Version of the English Bible" in Stephens, ed., *Bible, the Reformation and the Church*, 143–144.

12   *Bible in English*, 313. With successive editions of the Geneva Bible, the notes underwent significant expansion. By 1599, the notes to the New Testament had been significantly increased with additions by Laurence Thomson, one of the original translators of the Geneva Bible. Thomson's annotations to the Book of Revelation came from the Huguenot author Franciscus Junius the Elder (1545–1602). See Berry,

With the death of Queen Mary in 1558 and the accession of her half-sister Elizabeth to the throne—"our Deborah" and "our Judith," as Edwin Sandys (1519–1588), one of the Marian exiles and a translator of the Bishops' Bible, called her[13]—there was no longer any doubt that England and Wales were firmly in the Protestant orbit. But as we noted at the beginning of Chapter 6, the question that now came to the fore was to what extent the Elizabethan church would be in line with the Reformed congregations on the European Continent. When it became clear that Elizabeth was content with a church that was something of a hybrid— committed to Reformation truth but tolerating a variety of things in its worship that were left over from the Middle Ages for which there was no biblical sanction[14]—the Puritans, many of them Marian exiles, made it their expressed goal to reform the Elizabethan church after the model of the churches in Protestant Switzerland, in particular those in Geneva and Zürich. And their Bible was the Geneva Bible.

It was, in part, because of this identification of the Geneva Bible with the Puritan party that the episcopal establishment promoted a new translation, the Bishops' Bible, which saw the light of day in 1568. Though accurate in much of its rendering of the Hebrew and Greek, the Bible was a massive disappointment. Derek Wilson explains: the Bible was "rendered in stiff, cold English. It lacked the fluidity, the warmth of the version which the close-knit group of exiles had infused into the Geneva Bible."[15]

The failure of the Bishops' Bible to replace the popularity of the Geneva Bible is well seen by comparing the number of editions of these two Bibles. Between 1560 and 1611, there over 120 editions of the Geneva Bible, with an edition every year from 1575 to 1618 (seven years after the appearance of the King James Bible). By comparison there were only twenty-two editions of the Bishops' Bible between 1568 and 1611.[16] It is noteworthy that it was the Geneva Bible that

"Introduction to the Facsimile Edition," 16–17.

13 *The Sermons of Edwin Sandys. D.D.*, ed. John Ayre (Cambridge: Cambridge University Press, 1841), 81.

14 Robert C. Walton, *The Gathered Community* (London: The Carey Press, 1946), 59.

15 Wilson, *People's Bible*, 69.

16 Berry, "Introduction to the Facsimile Edition," 14.

was the Bible of that premier Elizabethan and Jacobean wordsmith, William Shakespeare (1564–1616), not the Bishops' Bible.

A PURITAN PROPOSAL OF A NEW TRANSLATION

The accession of James VI (1566–1625) of Scotland to the English throne as James I was greeted by the Puritans with a deep measure of joyful expectation, for James had been raised within the bosom of the Church of Scotland, one of the most Reformed bodies in Europe. They wrongly assumed that a man with such a pedigree would be amenable to their theological and liturgical concerns, which were quite similar to those of their Scottish brethren. They were wrong. James was imbued with a deeply-rooted conviction of the divine right of kings, namely, that the monarch derives his political legitimacy from God alone and therefore cannot be held accountable by any earthly authority. As such he found the fundamental hierarchical arrangement of the episcopal Church of England much more to his liking than the more egalitarian presbyterianism of Scotland, which was far more difficult for a monarch with James' convictions to control.[17] As James said early on in his reign in England, presbyterianism "agreeth as well with a monarchy as God and the devil"![18] Nevertheless, when James was presented with a list of Puritan grievances in what has come to be called the Millenary Petition (1603) at the very outset of his reign, he agreed to listen to them at a duly-called conference at Hampton Court near London in January, 1604.[19]

Four moderate Puritans were invited to present the concerns of their fellows to the king: John Rainolds (1549–1607), president of Corpus Christi College, Oxford, who acted as the spokesman; Laurence Chaderton (1537–1640), master of Emmanuel College, Cambridge, a distinguished Hebraist and Greek scholar and also one of the great preachers of that era[20]; John Knewstubs (1544–1624), a Suffolk

---

17 Wilson, *People's Bible*, 80–81.

18 Cited Nicolson, *God's Secretaries*, 56, modernized.

19 For the Millenary Petition, see Lawrence A. Sasek, ed., *Images of English Puritanism: A Collection of Contemporary Sources 1589–1646* (Baton Rouge/London: Louisiana State University Press, 1989), 338–341.

20 The story is told of one occasion when Chaderton had been preaching for two hours, and fearing to tax his hearers' patience any more, he prepared to bring his

rector and Thomas Sparke (1548–1616), a minister from Lincolnshire. Also invited to the conference, which stretched over five days, from Saturday, January 14, to Wednesday, January 18, were nine bishops of the Church of England, including Richard Bancroft (1544–1610), the Bishop of London who became the Archbishop of Canterbury a couple of months later, and seven deans, one of whom was the famous Lancelot Andrewes (1555–1626), whose mastery of fifteen languages and a wealth of theological and ecclesiastical knowledge rightly earned him the reputation of being one of the most learned men in England. Andrewes would be among the KJB translators.

It needs noting that some of the bishops were actually good friends of their Puritan counterparts. Rainolds' oldest friend was there the first day of the conference, Henry Robinson (c.1553–1616), the Bishop of Carlisle, an evangelical Calvinist like Rainolds and the other Puritans. As Adam Nicolson has rightly noted, "there was more uniting these [two] men than dividing them."[21] Chaderton and Knewstubs used to regularly spend time with Andrewes when the three of them were students at Cambridge, and Chaderton was actually at one time Bancroft's best friend, though the latter was now rabidly opposed to the Puritanism represented by Chaderton.[22] In total, there were eighteen adversaries of the Puritan party at the conference. The odds were clearly stacked in favour of the episcopal opposition to the Puritans and, in the final analysis, none of the Puritans' concerns were really addressed. Although the king's dealings with the bishops could hardly be called mild, he was sternness itself with the Puritans. He later said that he had "peppered them" and forced them so to flee "from argument to argument" that none of them could answer him directly.[23] The total failure of the conference from the point of view of the Puritans led to the radicalization of certain figures in the movement, who became committed to congregationalism, despairing of any hope of

---

sermon to a close. The congregation, however, cried out, "For God's sake, sir, go on, go on!" Cited Wilson, *People's Bible*, 83. For Chaderton, see H.C. Porter, *Reformation and Reaction in Tudor Cambridge* (Cambridge: Cambridge University Press, 1958), 239–241 and Nicolson, *God's Secretaries*, 130–131.

21 Nicolson, *God's Secretaries*, 45.

22 Nicolson, *God's Secretaries*, 45–46.

23 Cited Nicolson, *God's Secretaries*, 54, modernized.

further magisterial reform.[24]

It was on the second day of the conference, Monday, January 16, as the mid-winter sun was going down in the afternoon, that Rainolds proposed that there be "one only translation of the Bible to be authentic and read in the churches."[25] This seems a surprising proposal, coming as it did from a Puritan who would have been expected to have been content with the Geneva Bible, so beloved of the Puritan party. Adam Nicolson plausibly suggests Rainolds might have had in mind a revision of the Bishops' Bible, which Elizabeth I, had promoted as the official Bible of the English church, and which, despite the sumptuousness of its printed appearance, had never been popular with either the people or the Puritans, as already noted. Moreover, it was undoubtedly the poorest translation overall of the Tudor Bibles.[26] On the other hand, David Daniell, followed by Derek Wilson, believes that Rainolds was thinking of the advances that had been made in Hebrew and Greek scholarship over the fifty years that lay between his proposal and the publication of the Geneva Bible and that this alone necessitated a new work.[27]

Whatever Rainolds' motivation, James leapt upon the new proposal with zest, for he despised the Puritans' Geneva Bible. This had been the version that his redoubtable tutor, George Buchanan (1506–1582), had drilled into him when he was a young boy.[28] It was also this version that was favoured by the Scottish presbytery, of whom James was not

---

24 Daniell, *Bible in English*, 432. See Nicolson, *God's Secretaries*, 42–61, for the details of the conference.

25 Cited Nicolson, *God's Secretaries*, 57, modernized.

26 On the Bishops' Bible, see Daniell, *Bible in English*, 338–347.

27 Daniell, *Bible in English*, 435–436; Wilson, *People's Bible*, 86–87. Either Nicolson's suggestion or that of Daniell would answer the query of Leland Ryken: "Why did the Puritans ask for a new translation of the Bible when their preferred Bible—the Genevan—was the well-established best seller of its day?" [*The Legacy of the King James Bible. Celebrating 400 Years of the Most Influential English Translation* (Wheaton: Crossway, 2011), 46].

28 On Buchanan and his tutelage of the young King James, see the recent popular sketch in David Teems, *Majestie: The King Behind the King James Bible* (Nashville: Thomas Nelson, 2010), 40–49.

enamoured, as has been seen.[29] At a number of places this translation challenged his concept of an absolute monarchy. The word "tyrant," for instance, appeared around thirty times in the 1599 edition of the Geneva Bible. It is not found even once in the version that James would authorize.[30] Then, in the notes accompanying the text of Exodus 1, the midwives are commended for their disobedience of Pharaoh's command to kill the newborn Hebrew males at birth. "Their disobedience herein was lawful," the note to verse 19 read, though their lying to Pharaoh to cover up their disobedience was plainly designated as "evil." It should occasion no surprise that, in the list of guidelines for the new translation James would specify that "no marginal notes at all [were] to be affixed" to the text except those that were absolutely necessary for the explanation of the underlying Hebrew or Greek.[31]

TRANSLATING FOR KING JAMES

In the days following the Hampton Court conference, six panels of translators were appointed: two to work at Westminster on Genesis through to 2 Kings and on the letters of the New Testament; two at Cambridge University on 1 Chronicles to the Song of Songs and on the Apocrypha; and two at Oxford University translating the prophets as well as the Gospels, Acts and Revelation. There is no scholarly consensus about the total number of those involved first in translating and then in editing and revising. Of scholars writing recently on the history of the KJB, Alister McGrath lists forty-seven actual translators, while Gordon Campbell's list, which includes those involved in the later stages of revision, comes in at fifty-seven.[32] Of these, there were

---

29 Hall, "The Genevan Version of the English Bible" in Stephens, ed., *The Bible, the Reformation and the Church*, 125–126.

30 Nicolson, *God's Secretaries*, 58, alerted me to this fact, though he claims that "tyrant" "occurs over 400 times" in the text of the Geneva Bible. A search of a PDF of the 1599 edition yielded only thirty or so occurrences. Is he referring to the text of the original 1560 edition?

31 For all of the guidelines, see David Norton, *A Textual History of The King James Bible* (Cambridge: Cambridge University Press, 2005), 7–8.

32 Alister McGrath, *In the Beginning* (London: Hodder and Stoughton, 2001), 178–182; Gordon Campbell, *Bible: The Story of the King James Version 1611–2011* (Oxford: Oxford University Press, 2010), 276–293. For the division of labour among the six

only half a dozen or so, including Rainolds and Chaderton, who were clearly Puritan in their sympathies. Moreover, they were, for the most part, seasoned scholars. In the words of Gordon Campbell, "the learning embodied in the men of these six companies is daunting."[33]

James I actually wanted the Bishops' Bible retained as the standard, and the new translation more of a revision than actual translation. The royal printer, Robert Barker (d.1645), thus provided forty copies of the 1602 printing of the Bishops' Bible for the use of the translators.[34] As it turned out, though, the KJB was very much a fresh translation with the major literary influence, as has been observed, being that of Tyndale and not the Bishops' Bible.

Each of the six companies worked separately at first on the portion of the Bible assigned to it. Historians have only the sparsest of details about exactly how the translators carried out their work—it is still quite "mysterious," is the way that David Norton puts it.[35] Part of the evidence about the work of translation is a list of fifteen instructions drawn up by Bancroft as essential guidelines for the six companies. The close use of the Bishops' Bible as an exemplar was the first of these instructions, although the fourteenth directive allowed the translators to look at other earlier translations, including Tyndale's and the Geneva Bible. There is every indication that the other instructions were also carefully observed.[36] For instance, Bancroft had instructed the translators to keep "the old ecclesiastical words," so that "the word *church*" was "not to be translated *congregation*." This is obviously a rejection of Tyndale's preferred way of translating ἐκκλησία. As a result, although the word congregation is frequently used for the people of God in the Old Testament, it is never used for the church in the New Testament.[37]

---

companies, see McGrath, *In the Beginning*, 178–182; Wilson, *People's Bible*, 92. It is interesting that virtually all of those involved in the translation were from the south of England (McGrath, *In the Beginning*, 182).

33 Campbell, *Bible*, 55.

34 Campbell, *Bible*, 56–57. On certain peculiarities of the Bishops' Bible, see Norton, *Textual History*, 35–36.

35 For the sources available, see Norton, *Textual History*, 11–28. For the quote, see Norton, *Textual History*, 27.

36 For the list, see Campbell, *Bible*, 35–42.

37 The sole instance of the term in the New Testament is in Acts 13:43.

But observance of this instruction was also a way of rejecting some elements of Puritan theology, as Miles Smith's "Preface" noted: "we have…avoided the scrupulosity of the Puritans, who leave the old ecclesiastical words, and betake them to other, as when they put *washing* for *baptism* and *congregation* instead of *church*."[38]

Work on the translation had definitely begun by August 1604, and all of the companies seemed to have completed their assignments by 1608. These initial drafts were then vetted in 1610 over a period of nine months by a special review committee of between six and twelve men that met in London. We know the names of only three, possibly four, of the individuals on this review committee.[39] One of them was John Bois (1560–1643), a former fellow of St John's College, Cambridge, whose notes from the discussions of the committee of revisers are the only ones extant and which will be discussed in more detail below.[40] The work of this committee then went through the hands of two more men, one of whom was Miles Smith, who wrote the "Preface" to the KJB. Finally it was looked over by Archbishop Bancroft. So, towards the close of 1610, the manuscript was given to the royal printer, Robert Barker, to print.[41]

JOHN BOIS' NOTEBOOKS

A fascinating glimpse into the mechanics of the revision committee is provided by the notes of John Bois, which were long thought lost, but two copies of which have been discovered by Ward Allen and David Norton in 1969 and 1996 respectively.[42] Bois had been reading

---

38 "Preface to the Authorised (King James) Version, 1611," par. 15, Bray, *Translating the Bible*, 234.

39 For the chronology, see Anthony Walker, *The Life of that famous Grecian Mr. John Bois* 5.8–9 in Ward Allen, trans. and ed., *Translating for King James* (Nashville: Vanderbilt University Press, 1969), 139–140; Campbell, *Bible*, 61.

40 For these notes, see Allen, trans. and ed., *Translating for King James*, 36–113. For a discussion of Bois and his notes, see also Nicolson, *God's Secretaries*, 201–215. Nicolson suggests that Bois served as the committee's amanuensis and that his notes might have been the only ones written down (*God's Secretaries*, 208–209).

41 On Barker, see McGrath, *In the Beginning*, 197–199 and Daniell, *Bible in English*, 452–455.

42 Campbell, *Bible*, 64.

Greek and Hebrew from the age of at least six, having been tutored by his father. Not surprisingly, by the time that he studied at Cambridge his knowledge of the biblical languages was extensive. After he married in 1596, he resigned his fellowship and took a small country parsonage in the village of Boxworth, eight miles north-west of Cambridge. He would ride over to Cambridge each week to work with the committee assigned the translation of the Apocrypha. And later, when the revision committee was assembled in 1610, Bois was asked to serve on it. Up to this point, neither he nor any of his fellow translators had received any financial remuneration for their labours, but during the course of the nine months that Bois was in London, he, along with the other members of the revision committee, was given thirty shillings per week.[43]

Bois' notes, taken down during the course of daily meetings, reveal the revisers discussing the various shades of meaning a word can have, making grammatical points and debating them, sometimes with great vehemence, but always striving to find translations acceptable to the majority of the committee. Few of the suggested translations in the notes appear to have made it into the 1611 KJB. One that did was Bois' suggestion at 2 Corinthians 7:1 that the Greek ἐπιτελοῦντες ἁγιωσύνην should be translated as "perfecting holynesse."[44] Another of Bois' suggestions that was adopted at this revision stage was the phrase "being knit together in love" from Colossians 2:2.[45] Often, though, Bois' wordings were passed up in favour of another, better rendering. When, at Titus 2:10, Bois wanted "no filchers," an Elizabethan slang term for a petty thief, the committee stuck with "not purloining"—both equally obscure words for today's reader.[46]

On occasion Bois included the suggestions of the other revisers. For example, Bois notes that Andrew Downes (c.1549–1628), who had been his Greek tutor at Cambridge, and who had been quite reluctant to spend nine months in the English capital, remarked that if the words about Christ in Hebrews 13:8 were arranged in this manner

---

43 Walker, *Mr. John Bois* 5.9 in Allen, trans. and ed., *Translating for King James*, 141.
44 Allen, trans. and ed., *Translating for King James*, 51.
45 Allen, trans. and ed., *Translating for King James*, 63.
46 Allen, trans. and ed., *Translating for King James*, 73.

"yesterday, and today the same, and for ever," then "the statement will seem more majestic."[47] His fellow committee members, though, went with "the same yesterday, and to day, and for ever." Adam Nicolson rightly observes that Downes' remark about the phrase appearing more "majestic" reveals a key aspect of the translation that the revisers wanted it to have beyond fidelity to the original and clarity, and that is majesty and grandeur of style.[48]

THE INITIAL RECEPTION OF THE KJB

The early printings of the KJB, David Norton observes, were challenging for the printer Robert Barker since he was under considerable pressure "to produce as much as possible as fast as possible."[49] Thus, early print-runs were marred by a variety of typographical errors, of which the most famous was probably the "Wicked Bible" (1631), so named because the word "not" was omitted from the seventh commandment of the Decalogue (Exodus 20:14), turning it into a positive admonition: "Thou shalt commit adultery."[50] A close runner-up to this typo has to be the one that occurred in a 1612 printing, the first octavo edition. Where the psalmist says, "Princes have persecuted me without a cause" (Psalm 119:161), this edition reads, "Printers have persecuted me without a cause." Norton thinks this must have been an "error" deliberately introduced into the text by a disgruntled employee in Barker's workshop![51]

Despite such typos as these, the episcopal establishment enthusiastically supported the new translation. They hoped it would help stem the tide of radical Puritanism and promote ecclesial unity.[52] The Puritan wing of the Church of England were not so enthusiastic, and they continued to support the printing of the Geneva Bible, the last edition of which rolled off the press as late as 1644. It would not be until the

---

47 Allen, trans. and ed., *Translating for King James*, 87.

48 Nicolson, *God's Secretaries*, 211–212.

49 Norton, *Textual History*, 64.

50 Daniell, *Bible in English*, 460.

51 Roger A. Bullard, "Zeal to Promote the Common Good (the King James Version)" in Lloyd R. Bailey, ed., *The Word of God. A Guide to English Versions of the Bible* (Atlanta: John Knox Press, 1982), 193; Norton, *Textual History*, 25, 74.

52 Wilson, *People's Bible*, 124.

early pastoral ministry of the Puritan John Bunyan (1628–1688) in the late 1650s that the KJB would begin to shake the hold of the Geneva Bible over the English Puritan community. In fact, it is fascinating to find a spiritual descendant of these Puritans, a London Baptist by the name of Richard Hall (1729–1801), using a 1578 edition of the Geneva Bible as the family Bible in the mid-eighteenth century.[53] The Geneva Bible long retained its hold on the mindset of those committed to religious radicalism.

The severest critic of the KJB, though, has to have been Hugh Broughton (1549–1612), possibly the most distinguished Hebraist in Europe and who expected to have been among the translators of the KJB but was passed over, probably because of his combative spirit and violent temper. In the 1590s, Broughton had tried without success to convince the Archbishop of Canterbury, then John Whitgift, to establish a committee of six scholars, including himself, to revise the English Bible.[54] He was sent a copy of the KJB almost as soon as it came off the press with the hope that he would give it a positive commendation. Vain hope! His response was a blistering eight-page pamphlet, which pointed out some of the faults of the new translation and which began thus:

> The late Bible…was sent to me to censure: which bred in me a sadness that will grieve me while I breathe. It is so ill done.…I had rather be rent in pieces with wild horses, than any such translation by my consent should be urged upon poor churches. …The new edition crosseth me, I require it be burnt.[55]

In the "Preface" attached to the KJB when it was first published, the author of this prefatory text, Miles Smith, commented about the ultimate reason for the translation of the KJB and what it would undoubtedly engender. It was "zeal to promote the common good" that

---

53 Mike Rendell, ed., *The Journal of A Georgian Gentleman: The Life and Times of Richard Hall, 1729–1801* (Brighton: Book Guild Publishing, 2011), 30–32.

54 Norton, *Textual History*, 5, n.2.

55 *A Censure of the late translation for our Churches* ([Middleburg: R. Schilders, 1611?]), [1, 3].

had led the translators to labour on the KJB. Such a zeal "deserveth certainly much respect and esteem," but if truth be told, Smith went on, it "findeth but cold entertainment in the world."[56] Broughton's diatribe therefore would not have surprised Smith and his fellow translators. But thankfully no one listened to Broughton; the KJB was not burnt; and, in the due course of providence, it became the version of the English Bible that made the English-speaking peoples a people of the Book.[57]

---

56 "Preface to the Authorised (King James) Version, 1611", par. 1, Bray, *Translating the Bible*, 203.

57 In fact, as Patrick Collinson has pointed out: "the English Bible became the prime text of the Reformation to an extent not seen anywhere else in Europe. A Victorian historian of the English people was able to say that by the lifetime of Shakespeare they had become the people of a book, the Book. Modern bibliographical research has borne out J. R. Green" [*The Reformation. A History* (New York: The Modern Library, 2003), 44].

8

"That secret refreshment"

The spirituality of Oliver Cromwell

I am a conqueror, and more than a conqueror,
through Christ that strengtheneth me.
—OLIVER CROMWELL[1]

In 1654, when the Puritan divine John Owen (1616–1683) was having
his treatise on the doctrine of the perseverance of the saints published,
he included—with the manuscript that was sent to the printer, Leon-
ard Lichfield (1604–1657)—a letter that he wished to be placed at the
head of the book. The letter was addressed to Oliver Cromwell (1599–
1658) and the central portion of it ran thus:

---

1   Thomas Carlyle, *Oliver Cromwell's Letters and Speeches with Elucidations* (New
York: Charles Scribner's Sons, 1897), 205. This chapter first appeared as "'That Secret
Refreshment': The Life of Oliver Cromwell (1599–1658)," *The Free Reformed Student
Journal* (Summer 2000). Used by permission.

In the midst of all the changes and mutations which the infinitely wise providence of God doth daily effect in the greater and lesser things of this world, as to the communication of his love in Jesus Christ, and the merciful, gracious distributions of the unsearchable riches of grace, and the hid treasures thereof purchased by his blood, he knows no repentance. Of both these you have had full experience; and though your concernment in the former hath been as eminent as that of any person whatever in these later ages of the world, yet your interest in and acquaintance with the latter is, as of incomparable more importance in itself, so answerably of more value and esteem unto you. ...The series and chain of eminent providences whereby you have been carried on and protected in all the hazardous work of your generation, which your God hath called you unto, is evident to all. Of your preservation by the power of God, through faith, in a course of gospel obedience, upon the account of the immutability of the love and infallibility of the promises of God, which are yea and amen in Jesus Christ, your own soul is possessed with the experience. Therein is that abiding joy, that secret refreshment, which the world cannot give.[2]

Owen here touches upon two critical aspects that need to be taken into account in any evaluation of the life of Oliver Cromwell: his remarkable rise to political power and his inner walk with God. In this chapter we begin with Cromwell's conversion, the foundation of what Owen calls "that secret refreshment" Cromwell enjoyed all of his life after he embraced God's offer of salvation in Christ. We then look at Cromwell's convictions regarding God's providence which undergirded his own understanding of his rise to power. Then we look at three aspects of his rule over the English nation: his promotion of heart-religion, his attempt to secure genuine liberty of conscience, and finally, his desire to establish a godly government.

---

2   *The Doctrine of the Saints Perseverance Explained and Confirmed* in *The Works of John Owen*, ed. William H. Goold, 1654 ed. (Reprint, Edinburgh: The Banner of Truth Trust, 1965), XI, 5.

A SPIRITUALITY ROOTED IN CONVERSION

Oliver Cromwell was born in Huntingdon, Cambridgeshire, in East Anglia, on April 25, 1599, the only surviving son of a gentleman, Robert Cromwell, who, in turn, was the younger son of a knight, Sir Henry Cromwell. Despite these connections to the gentry, Cromwell's early years were spent on the fringes of East Anglian landowners. British historian John Morrill has convincingly shown that Cromwell's status in 1640, when the alarms of civil war began to sound in England, was much humbler than has generally been assumed.[3] His social links appear to have been with what was called the "middling sort," urban merchants and working farmers. Exemplifying these connections is his marriage to Elizabeth Bourchier in 1620, the daughter of a successful London fur-dealer.[4] Moreover, Cromwell had significant financial problems during this period as well as being somewhat sickly. In the words of Morrill, he "spent the 1620s and 1630s in largely silent pain at his personal lot and at the drift of public affairs."[5] That such a man with little rank or standing would rise to the historical prominence that he later occupied is, even to the jaundiced, secular eye of many modern historians, nothing short of amazing. To Cromwell, it was only explainable by the sovereign hand of God.

As for the role of Christianity in his upbringing, it used to be assumed that he had received a thoroughly Puritan education at the hands of Thomas Beard (d.1632), the local schoolmaster.[6] In fact, as Morrill has now shown in some detail, Beard was the very antithesis of the Puritan pastor: a covetous man who lived in a grand style, with little interest in what was important to the Puritans, namely the ongoing reformation of the Church of England.[7] Nor is there any clear indication that his parents were strongly inclined towards Puritanism.[8]

---

3   John Morrill, "The Making of Oliver Cromwell" in J. Morrill, ed., *The Nature of the English Revolution* (London/New York: Longman, 1993), 118–147.

4   Barry Coward, *Cromwell* (London/New York: Longman, 1991), 10–12; Morrill, "Making of Oliver Cromwell," 119–123.

5   Morrill, "Making of Oliver Cromwell," 118.

6   See, for instance, Robert S. Paul, *The Lord Protector: Religion and Politics in the Life of Oliver Cromwell* (Grand Rapids: William B. Eerdmans Publ. Co., 1955), 24–27.

7   Morrill, "Making of Oliver Cromwell," 126–130.

8   Morrill, "Making of Oliver Cromwell," 134.

What we do know with certainty is that between 1628 and 1634 Cromwell underwent an evangelical conversion that would be the dominant influence over the rest of his life.[9]

Thankfully, we are not in the dark about the immediate impact of this conversion, for Cromwell discussed his experience in a letter to his cousin, Elizabeth St. John, in 1638.

> [T]o honour my God by declaring what he hath done for my soul, in this I am confident, and I will be so. Truly, then, this I find: That he giveth springs in a dry and barren wilderness where no water is. I live (you know where) in Mesheck, which they say signifies Prolonging; in Kedar, which signifies Blackness: yet the Lord forsaketh me not. Though he do prolong, yet he will I trust bring me to his tabernacle, to his resting-place. My soul is with the congregation of the firstborn, my body rests in hope, and if here I may honour my God either by doing or by suffering, I shall be most glad.
>
> Truly no poor creature hath more cause to put forth himself in the cause of his God than I. I have had plentiful wages beforehand, and I am sure I shall never earn the least mite. The Lord accept me in his Son, and give me to walk in the light,—and give us to walk in the light, as he is the light! He it is that enlighteneth our blackness, our darkness. I dare not say, he hideth his face from me. He giveth me to see light in his light. One beam in a dark place hath exceeding much refreshment in it:—blessed be his name for shining upon so dark a heart as mine! You know what my manner of life hath been. Oh, I lived in and loved darkness, and hated the light. I was a chief, the chief of sinners. This is true; I hated godliness, yet God had mercy on me. O the riches of his mercy! Praise him for me;—pray for me, that he who hath begun a good work would perfect it to the day of Christ.[10]

---

9   Morrill, "Making of Oliver Cromwell," 134–135. For the date, see Paul, *Lord Protector*, 38–41; Morrill, "Making of Oliver Cromwell," 134–135.

10   Carlyle, *Oliver Cromwell's Letters and Speeches*, I, 100–101. The best analysis of this text is found in Paul, *Lord Protector*, 37–38.

Oliver Cromwell
1599–1658

Credit: An engraving based on the Samuel Cooper miniature. From the frontispiece of Thomas Carlyle, Oliver Cromwell's Letters and Speeches with Elucidations *(New York: Charles Scribner's Sons, 1897), I.*

What is unmistakable about this Scripture-saturated text is that it records an unforgettable event. We are not told how, but Cromwell came to see that at the core of his being was darkness and a love of sin. So great was this love for sin that he found Paul's words in 1 Timothy 1:15 the most apt description of his state: he was "the chief of sinners." Cromwell's use of this phrase should not be taken to imply that he led the unrestrained life of a libertine before his conversion, for which there is no evidence.[11] But nor is it mere hyperbole. In the light of God's goodness and the riches of his mercy, Cromwell can but view his pre-conversion life as a sinkhole of sin.

In what is an otherwise fine study of Cromwell's faith, J.C. Davis makes the curious assertion that "Cromwell's private religious thinking and devotion are sparsely documented."[12] This is hardly the case, as is evident from many of his letters and speeches. These written texts reveal that his conversion gave him a profound understanding of God. For Cromwell, he is both a "great and glorious God," who alone is "worthy to be trusted and feared,"[13] and also a Father who is "merciful, long-suffering, abundant in goodness and truth, forgiving iniquity, transgression and sin."[14] These attributes were in full display in God's covenantal work of salvation in the death of Christ for sinners. The covenant that God makes with Christ for the elect is a unilateral covenant in which God "undertakes all, and the poor soul nothing."[15] The sovereignty of God in salvation thus becomes the sinner's place of rest, not only at conversion, but for the rest of his or her life. As Cromwell tells his son-in-law, Charles Fleetwood (c.1618–1692), in 1652:

[S]hall we seek for the root of our comforts within us; what God hath done, what he is to us in Christ, is the root of our comfort. In this is stability; in us is weakness. Acts of obedience are not perfect, and therefore yield not perfect peace. Faith, as an act,

---

11 Morrill, "Making of Oliver Cromwell," 134.

12 J.C. Davis, "Cromwell's Religion" in John Morrill, ed., *Oliver Cromwell and the English Revolution* (London/New York: Longman, 1990), 187.

13 Carlyle, *Oliver Cromwell's Letters and Speeches*, I, 358.

14 Carlyle, *Oliver Cromwell's Letters and Speeches*, III, 29–30.

15 Carlyle, *Oliver Cromwell's Letters and Speeches*, III, 29–30.

yields it not, but as it carries us into him, who is our perfect rest and peace; in whom we are accounted of, and received by, the Father, even as Christ himself. This is our high calling. Rest we here, and here only.[16]

Three years later he can again write to Fleetwood, and tell him that his salvation consists in this one thing: that "God is bound in faithfulness to Christ, and in him to us; the covenant is without [ie. outside of] us, a transaction between God and Christ." Thus, despite daily "sins and infirmities," Cromwell, like all other believers, can "have peace and safety, and apprehension of love, from a Father in covenant, who cannot deny himself."[17]

Cromwell has various ways of describing the experience of entry into and standing fast in this covenant. In his letter to Elizabeth St. John cited above, he uses the imagery of illumination: God converting the heart by giving light and so dispelling spiritual darkness. In other texts he can talk of the light of God's countenance being better than life.[18] Alongside this imagery of light, Cromwell also uses the images of heat and flame. Writing to his daughter Bridget in 1646, he tells her to "press on" after Christ and "let not husband, let not anything cool thy affections." He expresses the hope that Bridget's husband, his close confidant and fellow soldier Henry Ireton (1611–1651), will in fact be used to "inflame" her love for Christ.[19]

In other texts, the imagery is drawn from the realm of sense and taste. In a 1655 letter to Charles Fleetwood, for example, he depicts the activity of the enlightened soul as "leaning upon the Son, or look-

16 Carlyle, *Oliver Cromwell's Letters and Speeches*, III, 29–30. Charles Fleetwood had married Cromwell's daughter Bridget in June 1652, about six months after Bridget's first husband, Henry Ireton, had died. By the time that this letter was written, Fleetwood had been appointed the Commander-in-Chief of the parliamentary army in Ireland.

17 Carlyle, *Oliver Cromwell's Letters and Speeches*, III, 212–214.

18 Carlyle, *Oliver Cromwell's Letters and Speeches*, II, 306.

19 Carlyle, *Oliver Cromwell's Letters and Speeches*, I, 254–255. Henry Ireton was one of Cromwell's closest confidants, an important parliamentary general and political theorist who played a vital role in most of the key battles of the Civil War.

ing to him, thirsting after him, embracing him."[20] He is convinced that those who have "tasted that the Lord is gracious" will be "pressing [on] after [the] full enjoyment" of him.[21] Finally, in one of the most moving expressions of his faith, Cromwell sums up what conversion means for the believer. It gives the believer a lifelong passion to enjoy God in heaven. Writing to his brother-in-law, Valentine Walton (died c.1661), to inform him of the death of Valentine's son during the Battle of Marston Moor, he tells him that the Lord has taken his son "into the happiness we all pant after and live for."[22]

A SPIRITUALITY OF PROVIDENCE

In the letter from John Owen that was cited at the beginning of this chapter, Owen made mention of the providential ordering of Cromwell's life. As Owen told Cromwell: "The series and chain of eminent providences whereby you have been carried on and protected in all the hazardous work of your generation, which your God hath called you unto, is evident to all."[23] Now, this belief in divine providence was the bread and butter of the Puritanism of Cromwell's day. For instance, the early Elizabethan Puritan Richard Sibbes could state on the basis of Matthew 10:28–30 that God's "providence extends to the smallest things, to the sparrows and to the hairs of our heads; he governs every particular passage of our lives."[24] Similarly Cromwell could urge Robert Blake (1598–1657) and Edward Montagu (1625–1672), key naval commanders in the Cromwellian government, to rely wholeheartedly on God's providential care. It will be salutary, Cromwell writes, for them to submit all of their

---

20 Carlyle, *Oliver Cromwell's Letters and Speeches*, III, 212–214.

21 Carlyle, *Oliver Cromwell's Letters and Speeches*, I, 254–255.

22 Carlyle, *Oliver Cromwell's Letters and Speeches*, I, 187–189

23 *Doctrine of the Saints' Perseverance* (*Works*, XI, 5).

24 *Of the Providence of God* in *The Works of Richard Sibbes*, ed. Alexander B. Grosart, 1862–1864 ed. (Reprint, Edinburgh: The Banner of Truth Trust, 1977), V, 35. For this reference, I am indebted to Blair Worden, "Providence and Politics in Cromwellian England," *Past & Present*, 109 (November 1985): 60, an article that has been very helpful in understanding Cromwell's convictions about providence. Also helpful in this regard are H.F. Lovell Cocks, *The Religious Life of Oliver Cromwell* (London: Independent Press Ltd., 1960), 28–44, and Davis, "Cromwell's Religion," 186–188, 199–201.

affairs to the disposition of our All-wise Father; who, not only out of prerogative, but because of his wisdom, goodness and truth, ought to be resigned unto by his creatures, and most especially by those who are children of his begetting through the Spirit.... Indeed all the dispensations of God, whether adverse or prosperous, do fully read that lesson. We can no more turn away the Evil, as we call it, than attain the Good.[25]

Here, Cromwell is not so much discounting the place of human endeavours and abilities, as seeking to inculcate distrust in them and total reliance on God's sovereign out-working of his purposes in every moment of time. As Cromwell had written to Richard Maijor (1604–1660), the father of one of his daughters-in-law: "Truly our work is neither from our brains nor from our courage and strength, but we follow the Lord who goeth before, and gather what he scattereth."[26]

This passage from Cromwell's letter to Maijor was written in the midst of Cromwell's campaign in Ireland, undertaken in 1649 and 1650 to prevent an invasion of England by Irish troops loyal to the future king, Charles II (r.1660–1685). It reflects another key aspect of Cromwell's providentialism, namely, the conviction that often God reveals his providential will in military victory. Thus, after the Battle of Marston Moor in 1644, Cromwell wrote to his brother-in-law, Valentine Walton, that the victory was "a great favour from the Lord." He thus could urge Walton, "Give glory, all the glory, to God." Likewise, after the other major parliamentary victory in the first phase of the Civil War, the Battle of Naseby, in June 1645, Cromwell told William Lenthall (1591–1662), the Speaker of the House of Commons: "this is

---

25 Carlyle, *Oliver Cromwell's Letters and Speeches*, III, 247. Robert Blake was a firm Puritan. As Admiral of the Cromwellian Navy, he played a significant role in making the English navy an extraordinarily powerful force. In his early years Edward Montagu appeared to be a firm supporter of the more radical Puritans, namely, the Independents and the Baptists. By the 1650s, this support was waning. After Cromwell's death in 1658 and the rapid collapse of Richard Cromwell's government, Montagu quickly switched his allegiance to the royalist cause. Thus it was he who brought Charles II back from the Continent to England on board his flagship, the *Naseby*, later renamed the *Royal Charles*.

26 Carlyle, *Oliver Cromwell's Letters and Speeches*, II, 159–160.

none other but the hand of God; and to him alone belongs the glory."[27]

Cromwell's overall conviction about the sovereignty of God in all human affairs is certainly biblical and worthy of imitation. Yet, would we want to say that God is always on the side of the victors? Does victory always indicate God's approval? I suspect that few Reformed Christians today would be prepared to give an unequivocal yes to these questions.[28] It strikes this writer that a more biblical perspective is one that Cromwell expressed near the end of his life when, in the spring of 1657, it was suggested to him that he restore the monarchy in his person and become King Oliver I. After much prayer and apparent indecision, he rejected this offer. During his struggle to discern what exactly God wanted him to do, he said: "who can love to walk in the dark? But Providence doth often so dispose."[29] This statement is a clear assertion of God's sovereign involvement in every event of an individual's life and the history of a people. But it is also a recognition that those who confess this providential sovereignty are not always able to discern the exact path it is taking.

A SPIRITUALITY OF ACTIVISM

As Cromwell sought to be a godly ruler in the aftermath of the English Civil War, he embraced three goals that gave further shape to his spiritual vision that we wish to consider. First, there was his desire to promote heart-religion, a vital Christianity in which substance and the Spirit were central, not form and church structures. And then, linked to this, he sought to create an environment where there might be genuine liberty of conscience. [30] Finally, convinced as he was that righteousness exalts a nation, he sought to put in place a godly government.[31]

---

27 Carlyle, *Oliver Cromwell's Letters and Speeches*, I, 187–189, 214–215. William Lenthall was the Speaker of the House of Commons throughout what is known as the Long Parliament, which met from 1640 to 1648. For further examples, see Worden, "Providence and Politics," 67–70, 81–83.

28 See Geoffrey F. Nuttall, *The Puritan Spirit* (London: Epworth Press, 1967), 130–136.

29 Cited Nuttall, *Puritan Spirit*, 134, n.1.

30 Davis, "Cromwell's religion," 190–191.

31 Ruth E. Mayers, "Oliver Protector: A Godly Ruler?", *The Banner of Truth*, 434 (November 1999): 5–10.

One of the first texts that enunciates Cromwell's belief that Christianity is to be a "Christianity of substance, of the heart and spirit" comes from Cromwell's military experience in the Civil War. Writing to William Lenthall a few days after his New Model Army had executed a victorious siege of the city of Bristol in 1645, he said:

> Presbyterians, Independents, all have here the same spirit of faith and prayer; the same presence and answer; they agree here, have no names of difference: pity it is it should be otherwise anywhere! All that believe, have the real unity, which is most glorious, because inward and spiritual, in the Body, and to the Head. As for being united in forms, commonly called Uniformity, every Christian will for peace-sake study and do, as far as conscience will permit; and from brethren in things of the mind we look for no compulsion, but that of light and reason.[32]

For Cromwell, all believers possess a genuine unity since, each is indwelt by the Spirit of God. This unity is the one that ultimately matters in the light of eternity, for it speaks of union with the head of the church, namely Christ. Cromwell is not prepared to say that unity in external matters, such as forms of worship and church government, so-called uniformity, is meaningless. These are matters about which Christians should pray for light and with regard to which they need to discuss and reason together. But, in Cromwell's mind, they are not issues over which Christian brothers and sisters should divide.

Thus, when Cromwell was appointed Lord Protector in 1653, it is completely understandable that he sought to create a climate that would make room for the differences of conviction between professing Christians. Scholars differ as to the exact parameters of Cromwell's policy of religious toleration and all of the motives that guided him in this regard.[33] There is, however, little gainsaying the plain fact that

---

32 Carlyle, *Oliver Cromwell's Letters and Speeches*, I, 228.

33 See, for instance, Paul, *Lord Protector*, 324–333; Cocks, *Religious Life of Oliver Cromwell*, 45–63; George A. Drake, "Oliver Cromwell and the Quest for Religious Toleration" in Jerald C. Brauer, ed., *The Impact of the Church Upon Its Culture* (Chicago: The University of Chicago Press, 1968), 267–291; Roger Howell, Jr., "Cromwell and

Cromwell had a burning desire for an atmosphere of religious toleration that precious few in his day were willing to sanction. He deplored the bitterness with which Christians often assailed one another and hoped that "every one, instead of contending, would justify his form by love and meekness."[34] If unity between the various groups of Christians was not immediately possible, however, Cromwell was then convinced that a second best was liberty of conscience.[35]

Like the rest of his fellow Puritans, Cromwell was convinced that the main means of converting men and women to Christ was the faithful preaching of the Word. But he also hoped that godly government would help in this regard.[36] In the words of Ruth Mayers:

> Cromwell mourned "the dissoluteness...in the nation" not simply because it contravened his personal morality, but because it offended the holy God, whose standards Scripture plainly set forth. At times, he grew weary of the burden of government and almost despaired of "doing any good." Yet the certainty that God alone could, and in his time would, impart genuine goodness enabled the Protector to overcome discouragements and persevere....Never did he lose the hope that "men of honest hearts, engaged to God...enlightened...to know his Word" might by precept and example do much to convince the disaffected of their errors and stem the 'current of wickedness'.[37]

CONCLUSION

What then is the legacy of Cromwell's life? Well, two things can be mentioned. First, in light of his emphasis on Christian unity, it is somewhat ironic that his major spiritual legacy was the three denomi-

---

English liberty" in R.C. Richardson and G.M. Ridden, ed., *Freedom and the English Revolution. Essays in history and literature* (Manchester: Manchester University Press, 1986), 25–44; Blair Worden, "Toleration and the Cromwellian Protectorate" in W.J. Sheils, ed., *Persecution and Toleration* (Oxford: Basil Blackwell for the Ecclesiastical History Society, 1984), 199–233; Davis, "Cromwell's religion," 191–199.

34 Carlyle, *Oliver Cromwell's Letters and Speeches*, III, 179–180.
35 Davis, "Cromwell's religion," 198–199.
36 Mayers, "Oliver Protector: A Godly Ruler?" 9.
37 Mayers, "Oliver Protector: A Godly Ruler?" 10.

nations that emerged from the splintering of Puritanism in the latter half of the seventeenth century—the Presbyterians, Congregationalists (or Independents) and the Baptists, the so-called Nonconformists and Dissenters.[38] This was a process that he helped along by giving these various groups the freedom to develop their own convictions. Oliver Cromwell's spirituality thus made a lasting impact on the shape of the Reformed community in Great Britain.

Second, Cromwell's life, and here I quote again from Ruth Mayers,

shows that much may be achieved by dedicated Christians dependent upon God, zealous for his glory and guided by his Word. Godly rule may be a thankless task, a constant uphill struggle, in which perfection is unattainable and temptations are multiplied. But earthly governments cannot be neutral in the conflict between sin and righteousness. Their policies will tend to serve either the one or the other....The example of Oliver Cromwell shows that Christian withdrawal from politics on the ground that no good can be achieved is an abdication of God-given responsibility which ensures the short-term triumph of ungodliness.[39]

---

38 Coward, *Cromwell*, 176–177.
39 Mayers, "Oliver Protector: A Godly Ruler?" 10.

9

"The Calvin of England"

John Owen and his teaching on biblical piety

The Puritan John Owen...was one of the greatest of English theologians. In an age of giants, he over-topped them all. C.H. Spurgeon called him the prince of divines. He is hardly known today, and we are the poorer for our ignorance.—J.I. PACKER[1]

Charles II once asked one of the most learned scholars that he knew why any intelligent person should waste time listening to the sermons of an uneducated tinker and Baptist preacher by the name of John

---

1   *A Quest for Godliness. The Puritan Vision of the Christian Life* (Wheaton: Crossway Books, 1990), 191. This chapter first appeared as "The Calvin of England: Some Aspects of the Life of John Owen (1616–1683) and his Teaching on Biblical Piety," *Reformed Baptist Theological Review*, 1, no.2 (July 2004): 169–183. Used by permission.

Bunyan. "Could I possess the tinker's abilities for preaching, please your majesty," replied the scholar, "I would gladly relinquish all my learning." The name of the scholar was John Owen, and this small story—apparently true and not apocryphal—says a good deal about the man and his Christian character. His love of, and concern for, the preaching of the Word reveals a man who was Puritan to the core. And the fragrant humility of his reply to the king was a virtue that permeated all of his writings, in which he sought to glorify the triune God and help God's people find that maturity that was theirs in Christ.[2]

In his own day some of Owen's fellow Puritans called him the "Calvin of England."[3] More recently, Roger Nicole has described Owen as "the greatest divine who ever wrote in English" and J.I. Packer says of him that, during his career as a Christian theologian, he was "England's foremost bastion and champion of Reformed evangelical orthodoxy."[4] But, as will be seen, Owen's chief interest was not in producing theological treatises for their own sake, but to advance the personal holiness of God's people.[5]

OWEN'S EARLY YEARS[6]

John Owen was born in 1616, the same year that William Shakespeare died. He grew up in a Christian home in a small village now known

---

2   For the story, see Andrew Thomson, *Life of Dr. Owen* in *The Works of John Owen D.D.*, ed. William H. Goold, 1850 ed. (Reprint, London: The Banner of Truth Trust, 1965), 1:xcii; Allen C. Guelzo, "John Owen, Puritan Pacesetter," *Christianity Today*, 20, no. 17 (May 21, 1976): 14; Peter Toon, *God's Statesman: The Life and Work of John Owen* (Exeter: Paternoster Press, 1971), 162. Subsequent references to the works of Owen will use the abbreviation *Works*, and are cited according to the volumes and page numbers of *The Works of John Owen, D.D.*, ed. William H. Goold, 16 vols., 1850–1853 ed. (Reprint, London: The Banner of Truth Trust, 1965–1968).

3   Guelzo, "John Owen," 14.

4   Guelzo, "John Owen," 14; Packer, *Quest for Godliness*, 81.

5   Guelzo, "John Owen," 15–16.

6   For a good account of Owen's life, see Toon, *God's Statesman*. For his theology, the best study is Carl R. Trueman, *The Claims of Truth: John Owen's Trinitarian Theology* (Carlisle: Paternoster Press, 1998). See also Sinclair B. Ferguson, *John Owen on the Christian Life* (Edinburgh: The Banner of Truth Trust, 1987); and Robert W. Oliver, ed., *John Owen—the man and his theology. Papers read at the Conference of the John Owen Centre for Theological Study, September 2000* (Darlington: Evangelical Press, 2002).

as Stadhampton, about five miles south-east of Oxford. His father, Henry Owen, was the minister of the parish church there and a Puritan. The names of three of his brothers have also come down to us: William, who became the Puritan minister at Remenham, just north of Henley-on-Thames; Henry who fought as a major in Oliver Cromwell's New Model Army; and Philemon, who was killed fighting under Cromwell in Ireland in 1649.[7]

Of Owen's childhood years only one reference has been recorded. "I was bred up from my infancy," he remarked in 1657, "under the care of my father, who was a nonconformist all his days, and a painful labourer [that is, diligent worker] in the vineyard of the Lord."[8] If we take as our cue the way that other Puritans raised their children, we can presume that as a small boy Owen, along with his siblings, would have been taught to pray, to read the Bible and obey its commandments. At least once a day there would have been time set aside for family worship when he would have listened to his father explain a portion of God's Word and pray for their nation, his parishioners and for each of them individually.[9]

At twelve years of age, Owen was sent by his father to Queen's College, the University of Oxford. Here he obtained his B.A. on June 11, 1632, when he was 16. He went on to study for the M.A., which he was awarded on April 27, 1635. Everything seemed to be set for Owen to pursue an academic career. It was not, however, a good time to launch out into the world of academe. The Archbishop of Canterbury, William Laud (1573–1645), had set out to suppress the Puritan movement, and to that end had begun a purge of the churches and universities. By 1637, Owen had no alternative but to leave Oxford and to become, along with many other Puritans who refused to conform to the Established Church, a private chaplain. He eventually found employ in the house of Lord Lovelace (1616–1670), a nobleman sympathetic to the Puritan cause. However, when the English Civil War broke out in 1642 and Lord Lovelace decided to support the King, Owen left his service and moved to London.

7   Toon, *God's Statesman*, 2.
8   *A Review of the True Nature of Schism* (*Works*, 13:224).
9   Toon, *God's Statesman*, 2.

A "CLEAR SHINING FROM GOD"

The move to London was providential in a couple of ways. First of all, it brought him into contact with the some of the leading defenders of the Parliamentary cause, Puritan preachers who viewed the struggle between the king and Parliament in terms of the struggle between Christ and anti-Christian forces. Moreover, it was during these initial days in London that he had an experience he would never forget. By 1642, Owen was convinced that the final source of authority in religion was the Holy Scriptures and moreover, that the doctrines of orthodox Calvinism were biblical Christianity. But he had yet to personally experience the Holy Spirit bearing witness to his spirit and giving him the assurance that he was a child of God.[10]

Owen found this assurance one Sunday when he decided to go with a cousin to hear Edmund Calamy the Elder (1600–1666), a famous Presbyterian preacher, at St. Mary's Church, Aldermanbury. On arriving at this church, they were informed that the well-known Presbyterian was not going to preach that morning. Instead a country preacher (whose name Owen never did discover) was going to fill in for the Presbyterian divine. His cousin urged him to go with him to hear Arthur Jackson (c.1593–1666), another notable Puritan preacher, at nearby St. Michael's. But Owen decided to remain at St. Mary's. The preacher took as his text that morning Matthew 8:26: "Why are ye fearful, O ye of little faith?" It proved to be a message that Owen needed to hear and embrace. Through the words of a preacher whose identity is unknown, God spoke to Owen and removed once and for all his doubts and fears as to whether he was truly regenerate or not. He now knew himself to be born of the Spirit.[11]

The impact of this spiritual experience cannot be over-estimated. It gave to Owen the deep, inner conviction that he was indeed a child of God and chosen in Christ before the foundation of the world, that God loved him and had a loving purpose for his life, and that this God was the true and living God. In practical terms, it meant a lifelong interest in the work of God the Holy Spirit that would issue thirty years later in his monumental study of the Holy Spirit, *A Discourse Concerning the*

---

10 Toon, *God's Statesman*, 12.

11 Toon, *God's Statesman*, 12–13.

John Owen
1616–1683

Credit: Steel engraving from volume 1 of Daniel Neal, The History of the Puritans or
Protestant Nonconformists; from the Reformation in 1517, to the Revolution of
1688 *(New York: Harper & Brothers, 1848), opposite 145.*

Holy Spirit.[12] As he later wrote: "Clear shining from God must be at the bottom of deep labouring with God."[13]

PASTORAL MINISTRY AND PREACHING BEFORE PARLIAMENT

In 1643 Owen was offered the pastorate in the village of Fordham, six miles or so north-west of Colchester in Essex. Owen was here till 1646, when he became the minister of the church at the market town of Coggeshall, some five miles to the south. Here, as many as 2,000 people would crowd into the church each Lord's day to hear Owen preach.[14] Thus, although Owen would later speak slightingly of his preaching to King Charles II—as seen in the anecdote with which this article began—it is evident that he was no mean preacher. It is also noteworthy that this change in pastorates was also accompanied by an ecclesiological shift to Congregationalism. Up until this point, Owen had been decidedly Presbyterian in his understanding of church government. His reading of *The Keyes of the Kingdom of Heaven* by John Cotton (1584–1652) which had been published in 1644, was decisive in changing his mind in this area of theology. It was also at Coggeshall that he wrote the classic work on particular redemption, *The Death of Death in the Death of Christ* (1647).[15] The backdrop for these early years of Owen's pastoral ministry was the English Civil War, when England knew the horrors of bloody fields of battle, and father was ranged against son and neighbour against neighbour on the battlefield. Well has this period been described as "the world turned upside down."

During those tumultuous days, Owen clearly identified himself with the Parliamentary cause. He developed a friendship with the rising military figure Oliver Cromwell and was frequently invited to preach before Parliament.[16] By late 1648 some of the Parliamentary

---

12 Toon, *God's Statesman*, 13.

13 Cited Peter Barraclough, *John Owen (1616–1683)* (London: Independent Press Ltd., 1961), 6.

14 Robert W. Oliver, "John Owen (1616–1683)—his life and times" in Oliver, ed., *John Owen*, 16.

15 For a study of this work, see Jack N. Macleod, "John Owen and the Death of Death" in *Out of Bondage* (London: The Westminster Conference, 1983), 70–87.

16 On Cromwell, see chapter 8.

army officers had begun to urge that Charles I be brought to trial on charges of treason since he had fought against his own people and Parliament. Charles was accordingly put on trial in January 1649, and by the end of that month, a small group of powerful Puritan leaders had found him guilty and sentenced their king to death. On January 31, the day following the public execution of the king, Owen was asked to preach before Parliament.

Owen used the occasion to urge upon the members of Parliament that for them, now the rulers of England, to obtain God's favour in the future they must remove from the nation all traces of false worship and superstition and wholeheartedly establish a religion based on Scripture alone. Owen based his sermon on Jeremiah 15. He made no direct reference to the events of the previous day nor did he mention, at least in the version of his sermon that has come down to us, the name of the king. Nevertheless, his hearers and later readers would have been easily able to deduce from his use of the Old Testament how he viewed the religious policy and end of Charles. From the story of the wicked king Manasseh that is recorded in 2 Kings 21 and with cross-references to Jeremiah 15, he argued that the leading cause for God's judgements upon the Jewish people had been such abominations as idolatry and superstition, tyranny and cruelty. He then pointed to various similarities between the conditions of ancient Judah and the England of his day. At the heart of the sermon was a call to Parliament to establish a reformed style of worship, to disseminate biblical Christianity, to uphold national righteousness and to avoid oppression. He assured the Puritan leaders who heard him that day that God's promise of protection to Jeremiah was also applicable to all who in every age stood firmly for justice and mercy.[17]

IRELAND AND OXFORD

Later that same year, Owen accompanied Cromwell on his campaign in Ireland, where he stayed from August 1649 to February 1650. Though ill much of this time, he preached frequently to "a numerous

---

17 *Righteous Zeal Encouraged by Divine Protection* (*Works*, 8:133–162); Toon, *God's Statesman*, 33–34. For help with this reference, I am thankful to Mr. Greg McManus of London, Ontario.

multitude of as thirsting a people after the gospel as ever yet I conversed withal."[18] When he returned to England the following year, he confessed that "the tears and cries of the inhabitants of Dublin after the manifestations of Christ are ever in my view." Accordingly, he sought to convince Parliament of the spiritual need of this land and asked:

> How is it that Jesus Christ is in Ireland only as a *lion staining all his garments with the blood of his enemies*; and none to hold him out as a *lamb sprinkled with his own blood to his friends*? Is it the sovereignty and interest of England that is alone to be there transacted? For my part, I see no farther into the mystery of these things but that I could heartily rejoice, that, innocent blood being expiated, the Irish might enjoy Ireland so long as the moon endureth, so that Jesus Christ might possess the Irish....If they were in the dark, and loved to have it so, it might something close a door upon the bowels of our compassion; but they cry out of their darkness, and are ready to follow every one whosoever, to have a candle. If their being gospelless move not our hearts, it is hoped their importunate cries will disquiet our rest, and wrest help as a beggar doth an alms.[19]

Although Owen's pleas were heeded and this period saw the establishment of a number of Puritan congregations—both Congregationalist and Baptist—in Ireland, Crawford Gribben has argued that the inability of the Puritans in Ireland to work together with like-minded brethren for the larger cause of the kingdom of Christ hindered their witness.[20]

By the early 1650s, Owen had become one of Cromwell's leading advisors, especially in national affairs to do with the church. There is little doubt that Owen was a firm supporter of Cromwell in this period.

---

18 *Of the Death of Christ* (*Works*, 10:479).

19 *The Steadfastness of the Promises, and the Sinfulness of Staggering* (*Works*, 8:235–236).

20 Crawford Gribben, *The Irish Puritans: James Ussher and the reformation of the church* (Darlington: Evangelical Press, 2003), 91–115.

As Owen told him on one occasion in 1654, for example: "The series and chain of eminent providences whereby you have been carried on and protected in all the hazardous work of your generation, which your God hath called you unto, is evident to all."[21] Two years later, though, when Cromwell was urged to become the monarch of England, Owen was among those who opposed this move. As it turned out, Cromwell did not accept the crown. But Owen's friendship with Cromwell had been damaged, and the two men were nowhere near as close as they had been.[22] This would have distressed Owen, since he had viewed Cromwell with enormous admiration.

Cromwell had appointed Owen to the oversight of Oxford University in 1652 as its Vice-Chancellor. From this position Owen helped to re-assemble the faculty, who had been dispersed by the war, and to put the university back on its feet. He also had numerous opportunities to preach to the students at Oxford. Two important works on holiness came out of his preaching during this period. *Of Temptation*, first published in 1658, is essentially an exposition of Matthew 26:41. It analyzes the way in which believers fall into sin. Central among the remedies to temptation that Owen recommends is prayer. His pithy remark in this regard is typically Puritan: "If we do not abide in prayer, we shall abide in cursed temptations."[23]

A second work, *The Mortification of Sin in Believers* (1656), is in some ways the richest of all of Owen's treatises on this subject. It is based on Romans 8:13 and lays out a strategy for fighting indwelling sin and warding off temptation. Owen emphasizes that in the fight against sin the Holy Spirit employs all of our human powers. In sanctifying us, Owen insists, the Spirit works

> in us and upon us, as we are fit to be wrought in and upon; that is, so as to preserve our own liberty and free obedience. He works upon our understandings, wills, consciences, and affections, agreeably to their own natures; he works in us and with us, not

---

21 *The Doctrine of the Saints' Perseverance Explained and Confirmed (Works, 11:5)*.

22 Oliver, "John Owen (1616–1683)" in Oliver, ed., *John Owen*, 26; Toon, *God's Statesman*, 97–101.

23 *Works*, 6:126.

against us or without us; so that his assistance is an encouragement as to the facilitating of the work, and no occasion of neglect
as to the work itself.[24]

Not without reason does Owen lovingly describe the Spirit in another
place as "the great beautifier of souls."[25]

Oliver Cromwell died in September of 1658, and the "rule of the
saints," as some called it, began to fall apart. In the autumn of that year,
Owen, now a key leader among the Congregationalists, played a vital
role in drawing up what is known as the *Savoy Declaration*, which
would give the Congregationalist churches ballast for the difficult days
ahead. Only a few days after Cromwell's death, Owen met with around
200 other Congregationalist leaders, including men like Thomas
Goodwin (1600–1680), Philip Nye (c.1596–1672) and William Bridge
(c.1600–1671),[26] in the chapel of the old Savoy Palace, in London. One
of the outcomes of this synod was a recommendation to revise the
Westminster Confession of Faith for the Congregationalist churches.
Traditionally Owen has been credited with writing the lengthy preface
that came before the *Savoy Declaration*. In it he rightly argued, antici-
pating a key issue over the rest of his life:

> The Spirit of Christ is in himself too *free*, great and generous a
> Spirit, to suffer himself to be used by any human arm, to whip
> men into belief; he drives not, but *gently leads into all truth*, and
> *persuades* men to *dwell in the tents of like precious faith*; which
> would lose of its preciousness and value, if that sparkle of free-
> ness shone not in it.[27]

---

24 *Works*, 6:20. See also the comments of J.I. Packer, "'Keswick' and the Reformed
Doctrine of Sanctification," *The Evangelical Quarterly*, 27 (1955): 156.

25 *The Nature, Power, Deceit, and Prevalency of the Remainders of Indwelling Sin in
Believers* (*Works*, 6:188). For further discussion of this area of Owen's teaching, see
Michael A.G. Haykin, "The Great Beautifier of Souls," *The Banner of Truth*, 242 (Nov-
ember 1983): 18–22.

26 For biographical sketches of these three men, see William S. Barker, *Puritan
Profiles: 54 Influential Puritans at the time when the Westminster Confession of Faith was
written* (Tain: Christian Focus, 1996), 69–94, *passim*.

27 "A Preface" to the Savoy Declaration in Philip Schaff, ed. and David S. Schaff,

The following year Owen preached again before Parliament. But the times were changing, and this proved to be the last of such occasions.

A LEADER IN A TIME OF PERSECUTION

In 1660 a number of Cromwell's fellow Puritan leaders, fearful that Britain was slipping into full-fledged anarchy, asked Charles II, then living in exile on the Continent, to return to England as her monarch. Those who came to power with Charles were determined that the Puritans would never again hold the reins of political authority. During Charles' reign and that of his brother James II (r.1685–1688), the Puritan cause was thus savagely persecuted. After the Act of Uniformity in 1662, which required all religious worship to be according to the letter of *The Book of Common Prayer*, and other legislation enacted during the 1660s, all other forms of worship were illegal.

A number of Owen's close friends, including John Bunyan, suffered fines and imprisonment for not heeding these laws. Although Owen was shielded from actual imprisonment by some powerful friends, he led, at best, a precarious existence till his death. He was once nearly attacked by a mob who surrounded his carriage.[28] At one point he was tempted to accept the offer of a safe haven in America when the Puritan leaders in Massachusetts offered him the presidency of Harvard. Owen, though, recognized where he was needed most.

The toil and anxieties of these years was accompanied by physical challenges, especially asthma and kidney stones. Mary, Owen's first wife, died in 1676. The following year, he married Dorothy D'Oyley, the widow of a wealthy Oxfordshire landowner whom Owen would have known from his connections to his home village of Stadhampton.[29]

But these years were also ones of great literary fruitfulness. His exhaustive commentary on Hebrews appeared between 1668 and 1684. *A Discourse Concerning the Holy Spirit* came out in 1674 and an influential work on justification, *The Doctrine of Justification by Faith*, in 1677.

---

rev., *The Creeds of Christendom*, 1931 ed. (Reprint, Grand Rapids: Baker Book House, 1983), III, 709. For a recent edition of this confession, see *The Savoy Declaration of Faith* (Millers Falls: First Congregational Church, 1998).

28 Barraclough, *John Owen*, 15.

29 Oliver, "John Owen (1616–1683)" in Oliver, ed., *John Owen*, 35.

Owen's *Meditations and Discourses on The Glory of Christ* (1st ed. 1684; 2nd ed. 1696), which Robert Oliver has rightly termed "incomparable," was written under the shadow of death in 1683 and represents Owen's dying testimony to the unsurpassable value and joy of living a life for the glory of Christ.

He fell asleep in Christ on August 24, 1683. His final literary work is a letter to a close friend, Charles Fleetwood, written two days before his death. "Dear Sir," he wrote to his friend,

> I am going to him whom my soul hath loved, or rather who hath loved me with an everlasting love; which is the whole ground of all my consolation. The passage is very irksome and wearysome through strong pains of various sorts which are all issued in an intermitting fever. All things were provided to carry me to London today attending to the advice of my physician, but we were all disappointed by my utter disability to undertake the journey. I am leaving the ship of the church in a storm, but whilst the great Pilot is in it the loss of a poore under-rower will be inconsiderable. Live and pray and hope and waite patiently and doe not despair; the promise stands invincible that he will never leave thee nor forsake thee.[30]

He was buried on September 4, in Bunhill Fields, where the bodies of so many of his fellow Puritans were laid to rest until that tremendous day when they—and all the faithful in Christ—shall be raised to glory.

A PIONEER IN BIBLICAL PNEUMATOLOGY

It is vital to realize that a concern for biblical piety lies at the very core of English Puritanism, of which Owen's theological *corpus* is a marvellous exemplar.[31] As was noted in chapter 6, Owen and the

---

30 *The Correspondence of John Owen*, ed. Peter Toon (Cambridge: James Clarke, 1970), 174.

31 Irvonwy Morgan, *Puritan Spirituality* (London: Epworth Press, 1973), 53–65, especially 60; Dewey D. Wallace, Jr., *The Spirituality of the Later English Puritans. An Anthology* (Macon: Mercer University Press, 1987), xi–xiv; Packer, *Quest for Godliness*, 37–38.

Puritans had inherited from the continental Reformers of the sixteenth century, and from John Calvin in particular, "a constant and
even distinctive concern" with the person and work of the Holy
Spirit.[32] Owen's pneumatology takes its start from the main pneumatological achievement of the ancient church, that which is found in
the credal statement of the Council of Constantinople in A.D. 381:
"[We believe] in the Holy Spirit, the Lord and Giver of Life, who
proceeds from the Father, who with the Father and Son is together
worshipped and glorified, who spoke through the prophets." Owen,
like other Puritan theologians, completely embraced as his own this
landmark statement of patristic pneumatology. For example, in his
A Brief Declaration and Vindication of the Doctrine of the Trinity he
declared that the

> first intention of the Scripture, in the revelation of God towards
> us, is…that we might fear him, believe, worship, obey him, and
> live unto him, as God. That we may do this in a due manner, and
> worship *the only true God*, and not adore the false imaginations
> of our own minds, it [that is, the Scripture] declares…that this
> *God is one*, the Father, Son, and Holy Ghost.[33]

And the Holy Spirit he affirmed to be "an eternally existing divine
substance, the author of divine operations, and the object of divine
and religious worship; that is, 'Over all, God blessed for ever.'"[34] Where
Owen, however, can claim to be doing pioneering work in biblical
pneumatology is the way in which he draws out the implications of
classical pneumatolgy for faith and practice.[35] Thus, Owen can rightly
state: "I know not any who ever went before me in this design of
representing the whole economy of the Holy Spirit."[36]

---

32 See chapter 6.

33 *The Doctrine of the Holy Trinity Explained and Vindicated* (*Works*, 2:377–378).

34 *The Doctrine of the Holy Trinity Explained and Vindicated* (*Works*, 2:399–400).

35 Geoffrey Nuttall, *The Holy Spirit in Puritan Faith and Experience* (Oxford: Basil
Blackwell, 1946), 7.

36 *A Discourse Concerning the Holy Spirit* (*Works*, 3:7).

OWEN AND BIBLICAL PIETY[37]

For Owen, genuine spiritual experience is vital. Owen asserts that ultimately it is the Spirit who gives the believer such experience: "He gives unto believers a spiritual sense of the power and reality of the things believed, whereby their faith is greatly established...."[38] It is these inner experiences that motivate external attendance on the various ordinances of the Christian life. "Without the internal actings of the life of faith," Owen writes, "external administrations of ordinances of worship are but dead things, nor can any believer obtain real satisfaction in them or refreshment by them without an inward experience of faith and love in them and by them."[39]

Inward experience of the power of God is especially important in the context of spiritual warfare, particularly the temptation to doubt God's existence:

Therefore the way in this case, for him who is *really a believer*, is, to retreat immediately unto his own experience; which will pour shame and contempt on the suggestions of Satan. There is no believer, who hath knowledge and time to exercise the wisdom of faith in the consideration of himself and of God's dealings with him, but hath a witness in himself of his eternal power and Godhead, as also of all those other perfections of his nature which he is pleased to manifest and glorify by Jesus Christ. Wherefore, on this suggestion of Satan that there is no God, he will be able to say, "He might better tell me that I do not live nor breathe, that I am not fed by my meat nor warmed by my clothes, that I know not myself nor any thing else; for I have spiritual sense and experience of the contrary"..."How often," will he say, "have I had experience of *the power and presence* of God in prayer, as though I had not only heard of him by the hearing of the ear, but also

---

37 Extremely helpful in summarizing Owen's teaching on biblical piety and pointing out key texts in this regard in Owen's massive corpus has been David M. King, "The Affective Spirituality of John Owen," *The Evangelical Quarterly*, 68 (1996): 223–233.

38 *A Discourse Concerning the Holy Spirit* (*Works*, 4:64). See also Owen's advice in a sermon that he preached on May 26, 1670: *Sermon XVIII* (*Works*, 9:237).

39 *The Grace and Duty of Being Spiritually Minded* (*Works*, 7:435).

seen him by the seeing of the eye! How often hath he put forth
his power and grace in me *by his Spirit and his word*, with an
uncontrollable evidence of his being, goodness, love, and grace!
How often hath he refreshed my conscience with the sense of
the pardon of sin, speaking that peace unto my soul which all the
world could not communicate unto me! In how many *afflictions*,
dangers, troubles, hath he been a present help and relief! What
sensible *emanations* of life and power from him have I obtained
in meditation on his grace and glory!"[40]

Similarly Owen can write elsewhere:

[L]et a gracious soul, in simplicity and sincerity of spirit, give up
himself to walk with Christ according to his appointment, and
he shall quickly find such a taste and relish in the fellowship of
the gospel, in the communion of saints, and of Christ amongst
them, as that he shall come up to such riches of assurance in the
understanding and acknowledgment of the ways of the Lord, as
others by their disputing can never attain unto. What is so high,
glorious, and mysterious as the doctrine of the ever-blessed Trinity? Some wise men have thought meet to keep it vailed from
ordinary Christians, and some have delivered it in such terms as
that they can understand nothing by them. But take a believer
who hath tasted how gracious the Lord is, in the eternal love of
the Father, the great undertaking of the Son in the work of media-
tion and redemption, with the almighty work of the Spirit creat-
ing grace and comfort in the soul; and hath had an experience of
the love, holiness, and power of God in them all; and he will with
more firm confidence adhere to this mysterious truth, being led
into it and confirmed in it by some few plain testimonies of the
word, than a thousand disputers shall do who only have the
notion of it in their minds. Let a real trial come, and this will
appear. Few will be found to sacrifice their lives on bare specula-
tions. Experience will give assurance and stability.[41]

---

40 *Grace and Duty of Being Spiritually Minded* (Works, 7:371).
41 *A Practical Exposition Upon Psalm CXXX* (Works, 6:458–459).

Here then is a strong emphasis upon an experiential Christianity, one that is rooted in the Spirit's application of biblical truth to the heart of the believer. It is this sort of spirituality, Owen argues, which provides assurance against doubt and ballast against apostasy.[42]

Now, one of the ways in which the believer grows in this area of biblical piety is growth in spiritual-mindedness. Indeed, Owen almost regards the striving to grow in spiritual-mindedness as a mark of conversion.[43] At the core of genuine spiritual-mindedness is meditation, reflection, both cognitive and affective. As Owen wrote:

> Spiritual affections, whereby the soul adheres unto spiritual things, taking in such a savour and relish of them as wherein it finds rest and satisfaction, is the peculiar spring and substance of our being spiritually minded.[44]

Truly biblical meditation aims at "the affecting of our own hearts and minds with love, delight, and humiliation."[45]

"THE BEATIFICAL MANIFESTATION OF GOD AND HIS GLORY"
As to the subject of meditation, Owen stressed that especially the person and work of Christ must occupy first place. "If we are spiritually minded, we should fix our thoughts on Christ above, as the centre of all heavenly glory," for it is in Christ that "the beatifical manifestation of God and his glory" is made for all eternity.[46] Owen would caution believers, though, that such meditation on Christ must be according to the Word. "In your thoughts of Christ," he declared, "be very careful that they are conceived and directed according to the rule of the word, lest you deceive your own souls" and do not allow your "affections to be entangled with the paint or artificial beauty of any way or means of giving [your] love unto Christ

---

42 See also *The Nature of Apostasy from the Profession of the Gospel and the Punishment of Apostates Declared, in An Exposition of Heb. VI.4–6* (Works 7:112–113).

43 *Grace and Duty of Being Spiritually Minded* (Works, 7:274).

44 *Grace and Duty of Being Spiritually Minded* (Works, 7:395).

45 *Grace and Duty of Being Spiritually Minded* (Works, 7:384).

46 *Grace and Duty of Being Spiritually Minded* (Works, 7:344).

which are not warranted by the word of truth."[47]

Owen is never slow to enumerate the blessed effects of such Christ-centred meditation. It will, he emphasizes, enable the believer "to endure all [their] trials, troubles, and afflictions, with patience unto the end." And it will transform the believer "every day more and more into the likeness of Christ." Thus, Owen can exhort his readers: "Let us live in the constant contemplation of the glory of Christ, and virtue will proceed from him to repair all our decays, to renew a right spirit within us, and to cause us to abound in all duties of obedience."[48] Thus, Owen concludes that such meditation

> will fix the soul unto that object which is suited to give it delight, complacency, and satisfaction. This in perfection is blessedness, for it is caused by the eternal vision of the glory of God in Christ; and the nearer approaches we make unto this state, the better, the more spiritual, the more heavenly, is the state of our souls. And this is to be obtained only by a constant contemplation of the glory of Christ…[49]

Some might feel that Owen's recommendations are unduly subjective. To this criticism, Owen rightly responds:

> I had rather be among them who, in the actings of their love and affection unto Christ, do fall into some irregularities and excesses in the manner of expressing it (provided their worship of him be neither superstitious nor idolatrous), than among those who, professing themselves to be Christians, do almost disavow their having any thoughts of or affection unto the person of Christ.[50]

One final text in this regard provides both a powerful indicator of Owen's own spirituality as well as a confirmation of the emphasis on piety among those to whom he preached and for whom he wrote. And

---

47 *Grace and Duty of Being Spiritually Minded* (*Works*, 7:345, 346).
48 *Meditations and Discourses Concerning the Glory of Christ* (*Works*, 1:460–461).
49 *Meditations and Discourses Concerning the Glory of Christ* (*Works*, 1:461).
50 *Grace and Duty of Being Spiritually Minded* (*Works*, 7:346).

it is a fitting conclusion to this chapter on some aspects of the life and piety of the "Calvin of England."

> The spiritual *intense fixation of the mind*, by contemplation on God in Christ, until the soul be as it were swallowed up in admiration and delight, and being brought unto an utter loss, through the infiniteness of those excellencies which it doth admire and adore, it returns again into its own abasements, out of a sense of its infinite distance from what it would absolutely and eternally embrace, and, withal, the inexpressible rest and satisfaction which the will and affections receive in their approaches unto the eternal Fountain of goodness, are things to be aimed at in prayer, and which, through the riches of divine condescension, are frequently enjoyed. The soul is hereby raised and ravished, not into ecstasies or unaccountable raptures, not acted into motions above the power of its own understanding and will; but in all the faculties and affections of it, through the effectual workings of the Spirit of grace and the lively impressions of divine love, with intimations of the relations and kindness of God, is filled with rest, in "joy unspeakable and full of glory."[51]

---

51 *A Discourse of the Work of the Holy Spirit in Prayer* (*Works*, 4:329–330).

10

"One brilliant shaft of light"

The marriage of Richard Baxter and Margaret Charlton

The meetest helper I could have had.
—RICHARD BAXTER

That marriage is a good estate and one ordained of God is a truth that Christians have never explicitly denied. Yet, there have been periods in the history of the church when there has definitely been a low regard for this vital institution. The fourth-century exegete Jerome (died A.D. 420), for instance, who was responsible for the Latin translation of the Bible known as the Vulgate, vigorously defended the view that celibacy was a vastly superior state to marriage, more virtuous, more pleasing to God. In Jerome's thinking, all of those closest to God in the Scriptures were celibate. In fact, Jerome argued, sexual relations between spouses were a distinct obstacle to leading a life devoted to the pursuit of genuine spirituality.[1]

Augustine (A.D. 354–430), another Latin-speaking theologian from the same era, whose thought provided the foundation for much of the thinking of the Middle Ages, similarly maintained that the celibate individual who devotes himself or herself to Christ is like the angels, and experiences a foretaste of heaven, for in heaven there is no marriage.[2] Why, then, did God ordain marriage? In Augustine's eyes, it was primarily for the procreation of children. Commenting on Genesis 2, Augustine was convinced that Eve would have been no use to Adam if she had not been able to bear children. What, then, of the biblical idea, found in this very chapter of Genesis, that the woman was made to be a delightful companion to the man, a source of comfort and strength? And what of the man as this for the woman? These ideas receive scant attention in the theology of Augustine.[3] In other works, Augustine argues that God instituted marriage for basically three reasons: (1) for the sake of fidelity, that is, the avoidance of illicit sex; (2) for the purpose of procreation; and (3) as a symbol of the unity of those who would inherit the heavenly Jerusalem.[4] These positions of Jerome and Augustine were largely embraced by the mediæval Roman Catholic Church.

SOME PURITAN PERSPECTIVES ON MARRIAGE

So it was that for many in western Europe, the Reformation was not only a rediscovery of the heart of the gospel and the way of salvation, long hidden under centuries of superstition and theological error, but also a recovery of the full panoply of ideas surrounding marriage in the Bible. After the death of his wife Idelette in March 1549, John Calvin for example, wrote to his fellow Reformer, Pierre Viret: "I am deprived of my excellent life companion, who, if misfortune had come, would have been my willing companion not only in exile and

---

1   J.N.D. Kelly, *Jerome: His Life, Writings, and Controversies* (New York: Harper & Row, 1975), 183, 187.

2   James A. Mohler, *Late Have I Loved You. An Interpretation of Saint Augustine on Human and Divine Relationships* (New York: New City Press, 1991), 71.

3   Edmund Leites, "The Duty to Desire: Love, Friendship, and Sexuality in Some Puritan Theories of Marriage," *Journal of Social History*, 15 (1981–1982): 384.

4   Mohler, *Late Have I Loved You*, 68.

sorrow, but even in death."⁵ This simple statement from one of the central figures in the Reformation, who was normally very discreet about his personal feelings, is a doorway into Reformation thinking about marriage—its innate excellence, its importance as a place of Christian affection and friendship, its role as a school of sanctification. The Puritans, heirs to the Reformers in this as in so many other things, faithfully transmitted this teaching about marriage, but also, as J.I. Packer puts it, gave it "such strength, substance, and solidity as to warrant the verdict that…under God…they were creators of the English Christian marriage."⁶

Like the Reformers, the Puritans strongly opposed clerical celibacy and affirmed that marriage is as intrinsically good as virginity, even hinting that it might be better. As Thomas Adams (fl.1612–1653), a renowned Puritan preacher, put it: "There is no such fountain of comfort on earth, as marriage."⁷ Similarly the Elizabethan Puritan author Robert Cleaver (died c.1613) could state: "There can be no greater society or company, than is between a man and his wife."⁸ The Puritans were very aware that marriage has other goods beyond the avoidance of fornication and its attendant evils.

William Gouge (1578–1653), a leader among London Puritans and a key participant at the Westminster Assembly, could repeat Augustine's view that God intended marriage for the procreation of children, but, he went on to emphasize, God also meant it for the mutual aid of

5   Cited Richard Stauffer, *The Humanness of John Calvin*, trans. George H. Shriver (Nashville: Abingdon Press, 1971), 45. On Calvin's marriage and thinking about marriage, see Michael A.G. Haykin, "Christian Marriage in the 21st Century: Listening to Calvin on the Purpose of Marriage" in Joel R. Beeke, ed., *Calvin for Today* (Grand Rapids: Reformation Heritage Books, 2009), 211–24.

6   J.I. Packer, "Marriage and Family in Puritan Thought" in *A Quest for Godliness: The Puritan Vision of the Christian Life* (Wheaton: Crossway Books, 1990), 259–260.

7   Cited C.H. George and K. George, *The Protestant Mind of the English Reformation 1570–1640* (Princeton: Princeton University Press, 1961), 268.

8   Cited Margo Todd, *Christian Humanism and the Puritan Social Order* (Cambridge: Cambridge University Press, 1987), 100. For further discussion, see Daniel Doriani, "The Puritans, Sex, and Pleasure," *Westminster Theological Journal*, 53 (1991): 128–129; Leland Ryken, *Worldly Saints: The Puritans As They Really Were* (Grand Rapids: Zondervan Publishing House, 1986), 41–42.

husband and wife. "No such help," writes Gouge, "can man have from any other creature as from a wife; or a woman, as from an husband."[9] As the Puritans reflected on Genesis 2, they disagreed profoundly with Augustine's reading of the text. God made Eve to be far more than the bearer of Adam's children. She was to be his companion, for, as Cleaver noted: "The husband is also to understand, that as God created the woman…so also he created her not of Adam's foot that she should be trodden down and despised, but he took her out of the rib, that she might walk jointly with him…"[10] It is thus not fortuitous that when that quintessential Puritan text, *The Westminster Confession of Faith* (1646), listed the reasons for marriage, this one of companionship comes in first place. "Marriage was ordained," we read in chapter 25.2, "for the mutual help of husband and wife, for the increase of mankind with a legitimate issue, and of the Church with an holy seed; and for preventing uncleanness."[11]

As Packer notes, Puritan preachers and authors are regularly "found pulling out the stops to proclaim the supreme blessing of togetherness in marriage."[12] For instance, Richard Baxter (1615–1691), whose experience of marriage is the subject for the rest of this chapter, could state:

> It is a mercy to have a faithful friend, that loveth you entirely, and is as true to you as yourself, to whom you may open your mind and communicate your affairs, and who would be ready to strengthen you, and divide the cares of your affairs and family with you, and help you to bear your burdens, and comfort you in your sorrows, and be the daily companion of your lives, and partaker of your joys and sorrows. And it is a mercy to have so near a friend to be a helper to your soul; to join with you in prayer and other holy exercises; to watch over you and tell you of your sins and dangers, and to stir up in you the grace of God, and remember to you of the life to come, and cheerfully accompany you in the ways of holiness.[13]

---

9   Cited Leites, "Duty to Desire," 387.

10   Cited Todd, *Christian Humanism and the Puritan Social Order*, 113.

11   On the significance of the order of reasons given for the institution of marriage, see Packer, *Quest for Godliness*, 261–262. See also Todd, *Christian Humanism and the Puritan Social Order*, 99–100.

12   Packer, *Quest for Godliness*, 262.

13   Richard Baxter, *A Christian Directory: or, A Sum of Practical Theology, and Cases*

Here Baxter speaks from rich and joyful experience. These words come from *A Christian Directory: or, A Sum of Practical Theology, and Cases of Conscience*, a "million-word compendium of Puritan teaching about Christian life and conduct,"[14] and were written in the mid-1660s, though the book was not published in its entirety until 1673. A few years before Baxter wrote these words he had married Margaret Charlton (1636–1681), one of his parishioners. Twentieth-century Baxter scholar, N.H. Keeble, well sums up their marriage: "Never minister had a better comrade....when all is said, it must have been, except that it was a childless union, as near an 'ideal marriage' as may be hoped of man and woman."[15]

THE SHAPE OF THEIR LIVES BEFORE THEIR MARRIAGE[16]

Richard Baxter's life spans much of the seventeenth century, one of the most decisive and turbulent eras of English history. He grew up in Shropshire, not far from Shrewsbury. As a boy and a teen, his formal schooling was negligible, which is noteworthy in view of the fact that

---

of Conscience II.1, in *The Practical Works of the Rev. Richard Baxter* (London: James Duncan, 1830), IV, 30.

14 J.I. Packer, "A Man for All Ministries," *Reformation and Revival Journal*, 1, no.1 (Winter 1992): 56.

15 "Richard Baxter's Love-Story and Marriage" in *The Autobiography of Richard Baxter*, ed. N.H. Keeble, abr. J.M. Lloyd Thomas (London: J.M. Dent & Sons/Totowa: Rowman and Littlefield, 1974), 274–275.

16 The best introduction to Baxter's life is the *Autobiography of Richard Baxter*. For an excellent biographical study, see Geoffrey F. Nuttall, *Richard Baxter* (London: Thomas Nelson and Sons Ltd., 1965). For brief biographical sketches, see J.I. Packer, "Great Pastors—V. Richard Baxter (1615–1691)," *Theology*, 56 (1953): 174–179 and *idem*, "A Man for All Ministries," 53–74.

The story of the love-relationship of Richard and Margaret is told by Baxter himself in his *A Breviate of the Life of Margaret, The Daughter of Francis Charlton, of Apply in Shropshire, Esq., And Wife of Richard Baxter* (London, 1681) and has been reprinted by John T. Wilkinson, *Richard Baxter and Margaret Charlton: A Puritan Love-Story* (London: George Allen & Unwin, 1928). More recently J.I. Packer has produced an abridgement of the Breviate: *A Grief Sanctified: Passing Through Grief to Peace and Joy* (Ann Arbor, Michigan: Servant Publications, 1997). For a helpful study of Baxter's overall theology of marriage, see Tim Beougher, "The Puritan View of Marriage: The Nature of the Husband/Wife Relationship in Puritan England as Taught and Experienced by a Representative Puritan Pastor, Richard Baxter," *Trinity Journal*, 10 (1989): 131–160.

Baxter is considered to be one of the most learned of the Puritan divines. He appears to have obtained his education primarily through reading, which was also one of the major means God used to bring him to a saving knowledge of Christ. Later, looking back as a mature Christian on the time of his conversion, he would state that he did not know when it actually took place, a fact that made him somewhat uneasy. Further reflection, though, led him to realize that "God breaketh not all men's hearts alike."[17]

Another formative influence on his Christian life was chronic ill-health that dogged him from his childhood. In 1671, when he was fifty-six, he recalled that from the age of fourteen, "I have not been a year free from suffering, and since twenty-two but few days, and since 1646 (which is about twenty-five years), I have had but few hours free from pain (though through Gods grace not intolerable)."[18] He was, in J.I. Packer's words, "a veritable museum of disease."[19] What was the effect of all this ill-health? First of all, it accustomed Baxter to think of himself as a man on the verge of eternity. This perspective gave him, in his words, "a deep sense of time's great preciousness."[20] Then, his physical problems produced in him a serious outlook on life. "The face of death, and nearness of eternity, did much convince me, what books to read, what studies to prefer and prosecute, what company and conversation to choose!"[21] Finally, it made him a serious and earnest preacher "I preach'd," he once remarked in an oft-quoted aphorism, "as never sure to preach again and as a dying man to dying men."[22]

At the age of twenty-three, in 1638, Baxter was ordained a deacon. For the next two years he served as the curate or assistant to the Anglican minister at Bridgnorth, Shropshire, a man by the name of William Medstard. He then moved thirteen miles south to Kidderminster, Worcestershire. This was the site of his most famous ministry, which took place between 1641 and 1661. When he arrived in the town the

---

17 Cited Nuttall, *Richard Baxter*, 6.

18 Cited N.H. Keeble, *Richard Baxter: Puritan Man of Letters* (Oxford: Clarendon Press, 1982), 11.

19 *A Grief Sanctified*, 43.

20 Cited Keeble, *Richard Baxter*, 12.

21 Cited Nuttall, *Richard Baxter*, 11.

22 Cited Keeble, *Richard Baxter*, 12.

majority of its inhabitants were, in Baxter's own words, "an ignorant, rude and revelling people,"[23] but this was to change dramatically. The face and soul of the entire community was revolutionized as a result of Baxter's ministry. He preached once a Sunday and once on Thursday, held a weekly pastor's forum for his flock for the purpose of theological discussion and prayer, distributed Bibles and good Christian books and personally catechized the 800 families in the town on an annual basis. Baxter can best describe the dramatic results of this ministry.

> The congregation was usually full, so that we were fain to build five galleries after my coming thither, the church itself being very capacious [it held up to a thousand people], and the most commodious and convenient that ever I was in. Our private meetings also were full. On the Lord's days there was no disorder to be seen in the streets, but you might hear an hundred families singing psalms and repeating sermons as you passed through the streets. In a word, when I came thither first there was about one family in a street that worshipped God and called on his name, and when I came away there were some streets where there was not passed one family in the side of a street that did not do so, and that did not, by professing serious godliness, give us hope of their sincerity.[24]

And the fruit of this ministry appears to have been genuine. It is fascinating to read a note that George Whitefield, the great evangelist of the eighteenth century, recorded in his diary on the last day of 1743 after a visit to Kidderminster: "I was greatly refreshed to find what a sweet savour of good Mr. Baxter's doctrine, works, and discipline remained to this day."[25]

---

23 Cited J.I. Packer, "Introduction" to *Richard Baxter, The Reformed Pastor*, ed. William Brown, 1862 ed. (Reprint, Edinburgh: The Banner of Truth Trust, 1974), 11.

24 *Autobiography of Richard Baxter*, 79. For an excellent study of Baxter's evangelism, see Timothy K. Beougher, "Richard Baxter and Puritan Evangelism," *Journal of the Academy for Evangelism in Theological Education*, 7 (1991–1992): 82–94. See also Gary E. Milley, "A Puritan Perspective on Preaching," *Resource*, 2, no. 3 (January–February 1988): 16–17.

25 Cited Packer, "Richard Baxter," 175.

Now, among those converted under Baxter's preaching at Kidder-minster was Margaret Charlton. Like Baxter she came from Shrop-shire—she had, in fact, been raised only a few miles from where Baxter grew up, though in considerably wealthier circumstances. She came to live in Kidderminster with her godly mother, Mary Hanmer (d.1661), who had been twice widowed and was delighting in Baxter's pulpit ministry. Initially, Margaret had little liking for either Baxter or the people of the town. She had, Baxter tells us in *A Breviate of the Life of Margaret, The Daughter of Francis Charlton, …And Wife of Richard Bax-ter, his account of their lives together*, a "great aversion to the poverty and strictness of the people" of the town. Frivolous and held by the gaieties of this world, she was far more interested in "glittering herself in costly apparel."[26]

The Holy Spirit, though, was at work in her life. A series of sermons that Baxter preached on the doctrine of conversion, which eventually found their way into print as *A Treatise of Conversion* (1657), was, Baxter tells us, "received on her heart as the seal on the wax." Her spiritual transformation was swift and genuine. As she later wrote:

> God hath…engaged me to Himself, by taking me into His Family, and planting me in His garden, and watering me with the dew from heaven.…I am Thine, Lord, and not mine own…Thou Lord that knowest all things, knowest that I have devoted my all to Thee.[27]

One of the first signs of this radical change in her life was "her fervent, secret prayers." She chose to pray in a portion of her mother's house that was not in use since it had been damaged during the Civil War. She naturally thought she could not be heard. But her praying was overheard by her mother and friends in the house. According to Baxter, they said, "they never heard so fervent prayers from any person."[28]

Not long after her conversion, which brought much rejoicing to many in the town, she was stricken with consumption and for a

---

26 Wilkinson, *Richard Baxter and Margaret Charlton*, 70.
27 Wilkinson, *Richard Baxter and Margaret Charlton*, 78, 81.
28 Wilkinson, *Richard Baxter and Margaret Charlton*, 107.

number of months her life seemed to be ebbing away. Baxter and a group of those whom he calls "humble praying persons" resolved to fast and pray for Margaret's healing. And God heard their prayers. The Lord, Baxter tells us, "speedily delivered her as it were by nothing."[29] At a public occasion in April 1660, when thanksgiving was made to God for her healing, Margaret acknowledged his great mercy to her and she declared that she was "taking Him only for my God and my chief felicity."[30]

At the time of this dramatic reversal of Margaret's ambitions and goals in life, there were also great changes sweeping the national scene. Oliver Cromwell, whose life and piety we looked at earlier in the book, and who had become the ruler of a republican England in the 1650s after nearly ten years of religious civil war, had died two years previously. During that civil war, the king, Charles I, had been executed as a traitor for making war on his own subjects, and his son, who would become Charles II, fled into exile on the European continent. After Cromwell's death, England seemed to be tumbling into anarchy, and the fateful decision was made by a number of Cromwell's former comrades-in-arms to restore the monarchy. Charles II stepped ashore at Dover on May 25, 1660, to a thunderous welcome. He was handed an English Bible, which he described as that which he loved more than anything else in the world. Subsequent events would cast doubt on the sincerity of this profession.

Coming to power with Charles was a parliament bent on breaking forever the political power and spiritual influence of Puritanism.[31] Those who had signed the death warrant of Charles I and were still surviving were quickly brought to trial and executed. The year after the restoration of the monarchy saw the first of a series of punitive measures against the Puritans, which would become known as the "Clarendon Code." Named after Charles' chief minister, they were

---

29 Wilkinson, *Richard Baxter and Margaret Charlton*, 73–74. Also see Packer, *A Grief Sanctified*, 21–22.

30 Wilkinson, *Richard Baxter and Margaret Charlton*, 75–77.

31 For an excellent study of the temper of these times immediately after the return of Charles II, see Geoffrey Robertson, *The Tyrannicide Brief. The Story of the Man Who Sent Charles I to the Scaffold* (New York: Pantheon Books, 2005).

aimed at all who would not conform to the rites of the Church of England. Particularly noteworthy is the Act of Uniformity, which came into effect on August 24, 1662. Roughly 2,000 ministers were ejected from their pulpits because they would not give unfeigned assent to everything in the *Book of Common Prayer*, which ordered the worship life of the Church of England. Among them was Baxter.

His precious ministry at Kidderminster was taken from him, and it was now illegal for him to preach or lead in worship—not only there but also anywhere in England. Shining in this time of darkness was "one brilliant shaft of light"[32]—his marriage to Margaret, which had taken place about two weeks after the Act of Uniformity came into effect.

THE SHAPE OF THEIR MARRIAGE

For various reasons, the marriage of Richard and Margaret became the talk of London. There was the difference in their ages, Richard being old enough to be her father. Then, there was the disparity in their social station, her mother's death in 1661 having given her considerable wealth. Finally, it was common knowledge that Baxter had advocated celibacy for ministers, due to their need to devote themselves unreservedly to their ministries.[33] While Baxter never affirmed the Roman Catholic view that the marriage of pastors was unlawful, he did caution those with a desire to oversee a flock:

> The work of the sacred ministry is enough to take up the whole man, if he had the strength and parts of many men....Believe it, he that will have a wife must spend much of his time in her conference, prayer, and other family duties....And if he have children, O how much care, time and labour they will require.[34]

32 Nuttall, *Richard Baxter*, 93.

33 *Autobiography of Richard Baxter*, 173–174; Wilkinson, *Richard Baxter and Margaret Charlton*, 109. But even after his own marriage he could urge ministers to think twice about getting married: Wilkinson, *Richard Baxter and Margaret Charlton*, 155–158; *Christian Directory* II.1 in *Practical Works*, IV, 20–22. See also Beougher, "Puritan View of Marriage," 152.

34 Cited Vance Salisbury, *Good Mr. Baxter: Sketches of Effective, Caring Leadership for the Church from the Life of Richard Baxter* (Nevada Ciy: Piety Hill Press, 2007), 82. This work has been quite helpful in orienting my thinking about Richard and Margaret's

Richard Baxter
1615–1691

Credit: Steel engraving from volume 1 of Daniel Neal, The History of the Puritans or Protestant Nonconformists; from the Reformation in 1517, to the Revolution of 1688 *(New York: Harper & Brothers, 1848), opposite xxiv.*

Once he was married, though, Baxter found that marriage agreed with him very well. As he wrote after his wife's death: "we lived in inviolated love and mutual complacency sensible of the benefit of mutual help. These near nineteen years I know not that we ever had any breach in the point of love, or point of interest."[35] Now, this statement needs to be read in light of the fact that neither Richard nor Margaret was an easy-going individual. Richard, a scholar and something of a recluse, was unpolished in social graces. He could be testy and his tongue sharp, a possible side-effect of regularly living in pain.[36] Margaret would gently scold him when he was careless or rash in his speech. Writes Baxter, "if my very looks seemed not pleasant, she would have me amend them (which my weak and pained state of body undisposed me to do)."[37] Baxter learned a valuable lesson about marriage through Margaret's correction of his faults. It was nothing less than a school of sanctification. As he advised husbands and wives in his *Christian Directory*:

'Conceal not the state of your souls, nor hide your faults from one another.' You are as one flesh, and should have one heart: and as it is most dangerous for a man to be unknown to himself, so is it very hurtful to husband or wife to be unknown to one another, in those cases wherein they have need of help. It is foolish tenderness of yourselves, when you conceal your disease from your physician, or your helpful friend; and who should be so tender of you, and helpful to you, as you should be to one another? Indeed in some few cases, where the opening of a fault or secret will but tend to quench affection, and not to get assistance from another, it is wisdom to conceal it; but that is not the ordinary case. The opening your hearts to each other is necessary to your mutual help.[38]

---

marriage. For access to this work I am indebted to Mr. Tim Challies, who loaned me his copy to use, and Mr. Chisso Wang, who delivered it to me.

35 Wilkinson, *Richard Baxter and Margaret Charlton*, 110.

36 Wilkinson, *Richard Baxter and Margaret Charlton*, 132, 135–136, 142.

37 Wilkinson, *Richard Baxter and Margaret Charlton*, 129.

38 *Christian Directory* II.7 in *Practical Works*, IV, 133–134.

Margaret, on the other hand, was often overwhelmed by obsessive irrational fears, nightmares and dread. Some of it was undoubtedly caused by nearly dying at least four times before she ever met Richard, as well as by an especially traumatic incident in the Civil War when her mother's castle was besieged, taken and sacked, and "men lay killed before her face."[39] And she too wrestled with a number of physical complaints, in particular, regular bouts of migraine and congestion of the lungs.[40] Moreover, she had "an extraordinary sharp and piercing wit," and was able to size up the character of men and women fairly quickly. She tended, Baxter tells us, to be quiet and reserved, and given her gift of understanding others, expected "all should know her mind without [her] expressing it." Not surprisingly, when people, including her husband, failed to understand what she was thinking, she felt frustrated.[41] Yet, unlike her husband, she had no struggles with anger.

Moreover, the circumstances in which they had been raised gave them quite different expectations about how to keep house, which undoubtedly caused some tension. Baxter writes of himself:

I had been bred among plain, mean [that is, humble] people, and I thought that so much washing of stairs and rooms, to keep them as clean as their trenchers and dishes and so much ado about cleanliness and trifles, was sinful curiosity, and expense of servants' time, who might that while have been reading some good book. But she that was otherwise bred had somewhat other thoughts.[42]

Years alone had made Baxter oblivious to the affairs of running a household. Eventually, though, he was happy to have one so efficient manage his affairs.

The Baxter household, like all but the poorest of the time, had servants. Margaret proved to be an extremely kind and caring mistress to

---

39 Wilkinson, *Richard Baxter and Margaret Charlton*, 106–107. See also Wilkinson, *Richard Baxter and Margaret Charlton*, 116–117, 134–135, where Baxter gives other reasons for her fearfulness.

40 Wilkinson, *Richard Baxter and Margaret Charlton*, 146.

41 Wilkinson, *Richard Baxter and Margaret Charlton*, 106.

42 Wilkinson, *Richard Baxter and Margaret Charlton*, 137.

them, almost always overlooking their faults and mistakes.[43] She insisted that Richard catechize them once a week and teach them from the Bible. On occasion Baxter would be so caught up in his studies that he would forget this duty. Margaret would then gently remind him with an expression of "trouble" on her face.[44] Servants in the Baxter home were treated as family: "She had an earnest desire of the conversion and salvation of her servants," Baxter wrote, "and was greatly troubled that so many of them (although tolerable in their work) went away ignorant, or strange to true godliness, as they came; and such as were truly converted with us she loved as children."[45]

They also lived in very difficult times when those who sought to order their affairs according to the Scriptures found themselves tossed into a furnace of persecution. Richard, known as a key leader among the Puritans, was dogged by spies, the frequent object of slander, and on at least one occasion arrested and imprisoned. They had to move house frequently and more than once lived in what could only be called wretched circumstances.[46] One gets a good idea of the nature of Margaret's mettle when Baxter tells us that at the time of his first imprisonment in 1669, Margaret "cheerfully went with me into prison; she brought her best bed thither, and did much to remove the removable inconveniences of the prison. I think she scarce ever had a pleasanter time in her life than while she was with me there."[47]

THE GOAL OF A CHRISTIAN MARRIAGE [48]

As one reads Richard's account of his marriage, there is little doubt of his and Margaret's deep respect for one another and their unbounded appreciation of one another's gifts and strengths. Baxter freely admitted that Margaret was better than he at solving problems relating to financial and civil affairs. "She would at the first hearing," he wrote, "understand the matter better than I could do by many and long

---

43 Wilkinson, *Richard Baxter and Margaret Charlton*, 132, 135.

44 Wilkinson, *Richard Baxter and Margaret Charlton*, 129.

45 Wilkinson, *Richard Baxter and Margaret Charlton*, 136.

46 Wilkinson, *Richard Baxter and Margaret Charlton*, 111–114.

47 Wilkinson, *Richard Baxter and Margaret Charlton*, 113.

48 Wilkinson, *Richard Baxter and Margaret Charlton*, 129.

thoughts."[49] Even when it came to practical issues of the Christian life, Baxter came to lean on his wife's wisdom.

> ...her apprehension of such things was so much quicker, and more discerning than mine, that though I was naturally somewhat tenacious of my own conceptions, her reasons and my experience usually told me she was in the right, and knew more than I. She would at the first hearing understand the matter better than I could do by many and long thoughts....Yes, I will say that...except in cases that required learning and skill in theological difficulties, she was better at resolving a case of conscience than most divines that ever I knew in all my life. I often put cases to her, which she suddenly so resolved, as to convince me of some degree of oversight in my own resolution. Insomuch that of late years, I confess, that I was used to put all, save secret cases, to her and hear what she could say....and she would lay all the circumstances presently together, compare them, and give me a more exact resolution than I could do. [50]

Thus, Richard could state: "I am not ashamed to have been much ruled by her prudent love in many things."[51] As Vance Salisbury rightly notes: Richard's marriage to Margaret

> reveals still another facet in Baxter's exceptional abilities as a shepherd and one which modern pastors may want to pay particular attention to; his spirit of humility and submission to others. With men, the relationship with their wives will often reveal the depth or shallowness of their humility and so, their suitability to the task of humble, servant leadership within the Body of Christ.[52]

---

49 Wilkinson, *Richard Baxter and Margaret Charlton*, 127.
50 Wilkinson, *Richard Baxter and Margaret Charlton*, 127.
51 Wilkinson, *Richard Baxter and Margaret Charlton*, 126.
52 Vance Salisbury, *Good Mr. Baxter*, 81. For a general admonition of husbands to be submissive at times to their wives, see Ephesians 5:21.

Margaret, in turn, recognized Richard's giftedness as a preacher. Despite the fact that it was illegal for him to preach, she regularly used large portions of her wealth to secure rooms for him to preach in. She even went so far as to pay for chapels to be built for her husband's ministry. A couple of instances that Baxter particularly recalled took place in 1673.

> At London, when she saw me too dull and backward to seek any employment till I was called…she first fisht out of me in what place I most desired more preaching. I told her in St. Martin's Parish, where are said to be forty thousand more than can come into the Church…where neighbors many live like Americans, and have heard no Sermon of many years.[53]

So she rented a large upstairs room where Baxter could preach on Sunday mornings and another minister could preach in the evening. During the very first meeting, the crowd of people seeking to hear Baxter was so great—there were close to 800—that the floor beam gave out a loud crack and then another, which "set them all on running, and crying out at the windows for ladders." Margaret Baxter pushed her way downstairs through the crowd and the first man she met, she asked what his profession was. He turned out to be a carpenter. He lived close by, and so he went and fetched a suitable prop for the beam. The next day they pulled up the flooring and found the beam was held by so slender a piece of wood that they "took it for a wonder that the house fell not suddenly." The building obviously could not contain the crowds attracted by Baxter's preaching. The fright of so many having nearly perished, Baxter noted, "increased my wife's diseased frightfulness; so that she never got off all the effects of it while she lived."[54]

Not to be defeated, however, Margaret set out to have a new chapel built from the ground up on a nearby vacant lot. Baxter preached the first Sunday after its completion, but was absent the following week, since he had to travel to a place about twenty miles outside of London. A Mr. Seddon, a preacher from the North of England—"an humble

---

53 Wilkinson, *Richard Baxter and Margaret Charlton*, 115–116.
54 Wilkinson, *Richard Baxter and Margaret Charlton*, 115–117.

pious man" is the way Baxter describes him—agreed to take Baxter's place and preach the next Lord's Day. State officials, though, had learned about the venture and were determined to arrest Baxter for illegal preaching. Getting a warrant for his arrest, they descended on the chapel. Not finding Baxter, though, they arrested Mr. Seddon in his stead and put him in prison for a number of months. Margaret felt Seddon's imprisonment keenly and blamed herself. She used her own funds to visit and comfort him in the prison, paid all of his lawyer's fees and also supported his family.[55]

There was a cost to all of this labour, and it was not merely material. It also brought, Richard writes, "trouble of body and mind; for her knife was too keen and cut the sheath. Her desires were more earnestly set on doing good, than her tender mind and head could well bear."[56] There were some, coming from the position that a woman's place is primarily in the home, who blamed Margaret for busying "her head so much about churches, and works of charity" and not being "content to live privately and quietly."[57] But Baxter defended her:

> …this is but just what profane unbelievers say against all zeal and spiritual godliness: what needs there all this ado? Doth not Paul call some women his helps in the gospel?[58] He that knows what it is to do good, and makes it the business of his life in the world, and knows what it is to give account of our stewardship, and to be doomed as the unprofitable slothful servant, will know how to answer this accusation.[59]

SOME CONCLUDING THOUGHTS

Richard and Margaret, like every married couple, were imperfect characters. As Richard said: "My dear wife did look for more good in me than she found, especially lately in my weakness and decay. We are all like pictures that must not be looked at too near. They that come

---

55 Wilkinson, *Richard Baxter and Margaret Charlton*, 118.
56 Wilkinson, *Richard Baxter and Margaret Charlton*, 132.
57 Wilkinson, *Richard Baxter and Margaret Charlton*, 124.
58 A reference to such texts as Philippians 4:3; Romans 16:2–3, 6.
59 Wilkinson, *Richard Baxter and Margaret Charlton*, 124.

near us find more faults and badness in us than others at a distance know."[60] And although the very trying circumstances in which they lived out their lives were more stressful than those that face most couples, all couples experience tension and stress. Yet, they managed to have a wonderful marriage. What was their secret?

Well, two things in particular stand out. First, Richard and Margaret followed the advice that Richard gave to married couple in his *Christian Directory*:

'Husband and wife must take delight in the love, and company, and converse of each other.' There is nothing that man's heart is so inordinately set upon as delight; and yet the lawful delight allowed them by God, they can turn into loathing and disdain. The delight which would entangle you in sin, and turn you from your duty and from God, is that which is forbidden you: but this is a delight that is helpful to you in your duty, and would keep you from sin. When husband and wife take pleasure in each other, it uniteth them in duty, it helpeth them with ease to do their work, and bear their burdens; and is not the least part of the comfort of the married state. "Rejoice with the wife of thy youth, as the loving hind and pleasant roe, let her breast satisfy thee at all times, and be thou ravished always with her love" [Proverbs 5:18, 19].[61]

But most importantly they had a tremendous agreement about what ultimately mattered in this life. "Suitableness in religious judgment and disposition," Baxter wrote as he drew his account of his marriage to Margaret to a close,

preseveth faster love and concord (as it did with us) than suitableness in age, education and wealth; but yet those should not be imprudently neglected. Nothing causeth so near and fast and comfortable an union as to be united in one God, one Christ, one spirit, one Church, one hope of Heavenly glory...[62]

---

60 Wilkinson, *Richard Baxter and Margaret Charlton*, 152.
61 *Christian Directory* II.7 in *Practical Works*, IV, 122–123.
62 Wilkinson, *Richard Baxter and Margaret Charlton*, 155. See also 128–129.

As Baxter was rightly convinced, at the heart of God's institution of marriage was that

> As the persons of Christians in their most private capacities are holy, as being dedicated and separated unto God, so also must their families be: HOLINESS TO THE LORD must be as it were written on their doors, and on their relations, their possessions and affairs.[63]

---

63 *Christian Directory* II.1 in *Practical Works*, IV, 1. I owe this reference and insight to Beougher, "Puritan View of Marriage," 134, 153.

11

"I will pray with the Spirit"
John Bunyan on prayer and the Holy Spirit

> When the Spirit gets into the heart then there is prayer indeed, and not till then. —JOHN BUNYAN[1]

Central to any expression of biblical spirituality is prayer. It is not surprising, therefore, that the Puritans, men and women who sought to complete the reformation in the Church of England and who sought

---

1   The bulk of this chapter has appeared in print as "'I will pray with the Spirit.' The Holy Spirit and Prayer in John Bunyan," *Kairos*, 2, no.1 (Fall 1988): 4–7; "The Holy Spirit and Prayer in John Bunyan," *Reformation and Revival Journal*, 3, no.2 (Spring 1994): 85–95; and "John Bunyan on Praying with the Holy Spirit" in Joel R. Beeke and Brian G. Najapfour, ed., *Taking Hold of God: Reformed and Puritan Perspectives on Prayer* (Grand Rapids: Reformation Heritage Books, 2011), 109–119. *The Reformation and Revival Journal* piece used by permission of ACT 3, P.O. Box 88216, Carol Stream, IL 60188 (www.act3online.com) and the article in *Taking Hold of God*, used by permission of Reformation Heritage Books.

to frame their lives according to God's Word,[2] wrote a great deal about this subject and were themselves, in the words of John Geree (c.1601–1649), "much in prayer."[3] As the Congregationalist theologian Thomas Goodwin remarked, "our speaking to God by prayers, and his speaking to us by answers thereunto, is one great part of our walking with God."[4] And given their deep interest in the Holy Spirit, the Puritans invariably rooted their discussion and experience of prayer in him and his work. A cluster of biblical texts—the description of the Spirit as "the Spirit of grace and supplication" (Zechariah 12:10), the admonition to both "pray in the Holy Spirit" (Jude 20; Ephesians 6:18) and pray for the Spirit (Luke 11:13), the experience of calling upon God as "Abba, Father" (Romans 8:15–16; Galatians 4:6) and that unique passage on the Spirit's intercessory work, Romans 8:26–27—were central in giving shape and substance to their reflections on this vital subject.[5] In this chapter, we will study what one Puritan, namely the open-membership Baptist John Bunyan had to say about prayer and the Spirit.

HISTORICAL CONTEXT

"Oft I was as if I was on the ladder, with the rope about my neck."[6] So John Bunyan reflected about his possible demise by hanging as he sat in a cold jail cell during the early 1660s. Bunyan's refusal to give up

---

2   The words of the Calvinistic Baptist William Kiffin (1616–1701), writing about a fellow Puritan and Baptist, John Norcott (1621–1676) are typical of Puritanism in general: "He steered his whole course by the compass of the word, making Scripture precept or example his constant rule in matters of religion. Other men's opinions or interpretations were not the standard by which he went; but, through the assistance of the Holy Spirit, he laboured to find out what the Lord himself had said in his word" [cited Joseph Ivimey, *A History of the English Baptists* (London: B.J. Holdsworth, 1823), III, 300].

3   John Geree, *The Character of an old English Puritan or Non-Conformist* (London, 1646) in Lawrence A. Sasek, *Images of English Puritanism. A Collection of Contemporary Sources 1589–1646* (Baton Rouge, Louisiana/Louisiana State University Press, 1989), 209.

4   *The Return of Prayers* in *The Works of Thomas Goodwin. D.D.* (Edinburgh: James Nichol, 1861), III, 362.

5   Roy Williams, "Lessons from the Prayer Habits of the Puritans" in D.A. Carson, ed., *Teach Us To Pray: Prayer in the Bible and the World* (Exeter: Paternoster Press/Grand Rapids: Baker Book House for the World Evangelical Fellowship, 1990), 279.

6   *Grace Abounding to the Chief of Sinners* 335, ed. W.R. Owens (London: Penguin Books, 1987), 81.

his God-given calling of an evangelist and preacher had led to his imprisonment in 1660, to his facing a possible death-sentence by hanging, and to his subsequent incarceration for twelve long years. When John Newton (1725–1807), the famous evangelical leader of the next century and the author of the well-known hymn "Amazing Grace," reflected on this difficult period in Bunyan's life, he noted that the "Lord has reasons, far beyond our ken, for opening a wide door, while he stops the mouth of a useful preacher. John Bunyan would not have done half the good he did had he remained preaching in Bedford, instead of being shut up in Bedford prison."[7] Now, what Newton probably had in mind are the two evangelical classics which came from Bunyan's pen as a result of this imprisonment from 1660 to 1672, namely, the account of his conversion which he entitled *Grace Abounding to the Chief of Sinners* (1666) and *The Pilgrim's Progress* (1678 and 1684). Down through the centuries, the vision contained within these two books has nourished believers and encouraged them in their pilgrimage. For instance, during the eighteenth century and the evangelical revival which dominated that period of time, these two works of Bunyan were read with great spiritual relish. As N.H. Keeble notes:

> Leaders of the Evangelical Revival and of Methodism were inspired by him (ie. Bunyan), returned to him often, and recommended him constantly. Howel Harris was a devoted reader. George Whitefield contributed a preface to the third edition of *The Works* (1767). John Wesley more than once read through *The Pilgrim's Progress* (and other Bunyan titles) on horseback, and himself abridged it in 1743...Methodist preachers made frequent reference to Bunyan, who exerted a formative influence on their own autobiographies.[8]

---

7   *The Works of the Rev. John Newton* (London: George King, 1833), I, lxxxv. In 1776 Newton had contributed notes to one of the first annotated editions of Bunyan's *The Pilgrims Progress, Part I*.

8   N.H. Keeble, "'Of him thousands daily sing and talk': Bunyan and his reputation" in *John Bunyan: Conventicle and Parnassus. Tercentenary Essays* (Oxford: Clarendon Press, 1988), 249–250.

There were, however, other works written by Bunyan during this long time of imprisonment, and though now not so well known, they are still deserving of consideration. One of the earliest of these works is *I will pray with the Spirit*, written around 1662.[9] It is a powerful plea to the religious authorities of his day to recognize the sovereignty of the Holy Spirit in the prayer-life of the believer and in the worship of the church. In what follows, the theological and historical contexts of Bunyan's treatise on prayer is outlined, along with the heart of its argumentation and its abiding significance.

THE THEOLOGICAL CONTEXT

When Bunyan was put on trial in January, 1661, he was accused of having broken the Elizabethan Conventicle Act of 1593 which specified that anyone "devilishly and perniciously abstained from coming to Church [ie. the Church of England] to hear Divine Service" and of being "a common upholder of several unlawful meetings and conventicles" could be held without bail until he or she agreed to submit the authorities of the Anglican Church.[10] In the eyes of the authorities Bunyan was an uneducated, unordained common "mechanic." It was made clear to Bunyan that he would be released if he promised to desist from preaching.

Bunyan, though, had a higher loyalty than obedience to an earthly monarch—obedience to King Jesus. Bunyan, like the majority of his fellow Puritans, believed in obedience to the laws of the state, and he emphasized that he looked upon it as his duty to behave himself under the king's government both as becomes a man and a Christian. But Bunyan knew that the Spirit of God had given him a gift for preaching, a gift that had been confirmed by the congregation of which he was a member. In Bunyan's own words: "The Holy Ghost never intended

---

9   For the date, see Richard L. Greaves, "Introduction" to R.L. Greaves, ed., *John Bunyan: The Doctrine of the Law and Grace unfolded and I will pray with the Spirit* (Oxford: Clarendon Press, 1976), xi–xii. Subsequent quotations from *I will pray with the Spirit* will be taken from this text, which is the latest critical edition. For a recent modernization and abridgment of *I will pray wth the Spirit*, see Louis Gifford Parkhurst, Jr., ed., *Pilgrim's Prayer Book* (Wheaton, Illinois: Tyndale House Publishers, Inc., 1986).

10   *Grace Abounding to the Chief of Sinners*, ed. Owens, 127, n.137.

John Bunyan
1628–1688

Credit: *Frontispiece in* The Complete Works of John Bunyan *(Philadelphia: Bradley, Garretson & Co., 1879).*

that men who have gifts and abilities should bury them in the earth."[11] For Bunyan, those imbued with the gifts of the Holy Spirit to preach had no choice but to exercise the gifts that God had given them. During his trial, Bunyan defended his right to preach by quoting 1 Peter 4:10–11. Those judging his case maintained that only those ordained by the Church of England could lawfully preach. Bunyan's disagreement was rooted in the fact that, for him, the ultimate authority in religious matters was not human tradition or human laws, but the Scriptures and their author, God. Bunyan had to obey his God, otherwise on the day of judgement he would be counted a traitor to Christ.

At his trial Bunyan had also been asked by Sir John Kelynge (d.1671), one of the judges, to justify his absence from worship in the local parish church. Bunyan, true to his Puritan heritage, stated that "he did not find it commanded in the word of God."[12] Kelynge pointed out that prayer was a duty. Bunyan agreed, but he insisted that it was a duty to be performed with the Spirit's aid, not by means of the *Book of Common Prayer*, which set out the structure for the worship services of the Church of England. Bunyan proceeded to argue:

> Those prayers in the Common Prayer-book, was such as was made by other men, and not by the motions of the Holy Ghost, within our hearts.…The scripture saith, that it is the Spirit as helpeth our infirmities; for we know not what we should pray for as we ought; but the Spirit itself maketh intercession for us, with sighs and groanings which cannot be uttered. Mark,…it doth not say the Common prayer-book teacheth us how to pray, but the Spirit.[13]

Bunyan's outright rejection of the use of written prayers cannot be understood apart from the view of his Puritan contemporaries and forebears.[14] John Calvin, the spiritual father of anglophone Puritanism,

---

11 *Grace Abounding to the Chief of Sinners* 270, ed. Owens, 68.

12 *A Relation of the Imprisonment of Mr. John Bunyan* in *Grace Abounding to the Chief of Sinners*, ed. Owens, 95.

13 *Imprisonment of Mr. John Bunyan* in *Grace Abounding to the Chief of Sinners*, ed. Owens, 95, 96.

14 For the following discussion of "prayer in the Spirit," I am indebted to Geoffrey F. Nuttall, *The Holy Spirit in Puritan Faith and Experience*, 2nd ed. (Oxford: Basil Black-

had defined prayer as essentially an "emotion of the heart…, which is poured out and laid open before God." At the same time Calvin was tolerant of written prayers. Some of his spiritual children among the English Puritans, like Richard Baxter,[15] preserved both of these emphases. Many of the Puritans, however, took Calvin's view of prayer to its logical conclusion and saw little need for written prayers.

Walter Cradock (c.1610–1659), a Welsh Congregationalist preacher and author, stated forthrightly: "When it may be the (poor Minister)… would have rejoiced to have poured out his soul to the Lord, he was tied to an old Service Book, and must read that till he grieved the Spirit of God, and dried up his own spirit as a chip, that he could not pray." John Owen, Bunyan's friend and admirer,[16] similarly maintained that "constant and unvaried use of set forms of prayer may become a great occasion of quenching the Spirit." Owen conceded that the use of written prayers is not intrinsically evil. But since the Spirit whom God had given to the believer is "the Spirit of grace and supplication" (Zechariah 12:10), the believer has all the resources that he needs for prayer. Moreover, Owen affirmed that the

> Holy Ghost, as a Spirit of grace and supplication, is nowhere, that I know of, promised unto any to help or assist them in composing prayers for others; and therefore we have no ground to pray for him or his assistance unto that end in particular.[17]

---

well, 1947), 62–74; A.G. Matthews, "The Puritans at Prayer" in A.G. Matthews, ed., *Mr. Pepys and Nonconformity* (London: Independent Press, 1954), 100–122; Horton Davies, *The Worship of the English Puritans*, 1948 ed. (Reprint, Morgan: Soli Deo Gloria, 1997), 98–161; Garth B. Wilson, "The Puritan Doctrine of the Holy Spirit: A Critical Investigation of a Crucial Chapter in the History of Protestant Theology," Th.D. Dissertation, Knox College, Toronto, 1978, 208–223; Alan L. Hayes, "Spirit and Structure in Elizabethan Public Prayer" in E.J. Furcha, ed., *Spirit within Structure: Essays in Honor of George Johnston on the Occasion of His Seventieth Birthday* (Allison Park: Pickwick Publications, 1983), 117–132. The texts cited from Calvin, Cradock and Owen are taken from these studies.

15 For Baxter, see chapter 10.

16 On Owen, see chapter 9. Owen helped Bunyan publish *The Pilgrim's Progress*. On his friendship with and admiration for Bunyan, see chapter 9.

17 *The Works of John Owen, D.D.*, ed. Thomas Russell (London: Richard Baynes, 1826), IV, 139.

These criticisms of the *Book of Common Prayer* accurately reflect Puritan dissatisfaction with both the type and content of the prayers in this book. Moreover, undergirding the approach of both Cradock and Owen to prayer was an intense interest in the work of the Spirit in general and the accompanying recognition that only with his empowering could God be rightly served and worshipped. Bunyan shares these perspectives on prayer and the Spirit, but states them in his own expressive way.

THE HEART OF BUNYAN'S TREATISE ON PRAYER

Bunyan's interest in extemporaneous prayer, quickened by his debate with Kelynge, found written form not long after his trial in *I will pray with the Spirit*. There are no surviving copies of the first edition. The second edition, dated 1663, appears without a bookseller's or publisher's name on the title page. The title page simply states "Printed for the author." The book was probably too hot for any publisher to handle![18] And no wonder when Bunyan declared near the end of the book: "Look into the gaols in England, and into the alehouses of the same: and I believe, you will find those that plead for the Spirit of prayer in the gaol, and them that look after the form of men's inventions only, in the alehouse."[19]

Bunyan's tract on prayer opens with a "definition" of prayer which is somewhat reminiscent of that of John Calvin:

> Prayer is a sincere, sensible, affectionate pouring out of the heart or soul to God through Christ, in the strength and assistance of the Holy Spirit, for such things as God hath promised, or according to the Word, for the good of the Church, with submission, in Faith, to the will of God.[20]

The rest of the book takes up each individual item in this "definition." Understandably, it is his discussion of the clause "in the strength and

---

18 Roger Sharrock, "When at the first I took my pen in hand": Bunyan and the Book" in Keeble, ed., *John Bunyan*, 80.

19 *I will pray with the Spirit*, 294.

20 *I will pray with the Spirit*, 235.

assistance of the Holy Spirit" which forms the heart of his treatise, for it was this very point that was in dispute. In discussing this clause regarding the Spirit's role in prayer, Bunyan takes his start from Ephesians 2:18 and Romans 8:26–27. On the basis of these Pauline texts, Bunyan asserts that "there is no man, nor Church in the world, that can come to God in Prayer but by the assistance of the Holy Spirit."[21]

Bunyan then proceeds to detail a number of reasons as to why the Spirit's aid is so vital when it comes to prayer. A consideration of the more important of these reasons brings the reader to the centre of Bunyan's plea that the Spirit be allowed full freedom to work in the lives of men and women.

First, only by the Spirit can a person think rightly of the One to whom he prays: "They then, not being able to conceive aright of God to whom they pray, of Christ through whom they pray…how shall they be able to address themselves to God, without the Spirit help this infirmity?"[22] Bunyan is emphatic that the *Book of Common Prayer* is of absolutely no help when it comes to the imparting of such spiritual understanding. The Spirit, and he alone, can reveal the Father and the Son as the proper recipients of prayer.

Second, only the Spirit can "shew a man clearly his misery by nature, and so put a man into the posture of prayer."[23] But such sensibility of sin would cause a man to flee from God's presence were it not for the Spirit's encouragement to run to God for mercy. Moreover, Bunyan stresses that only the Spirit can enable the believer to persevere in prayer once he or she has begun.

> May I but speak my own Experience, and from that tell you the difficulty of Praying to God as I ought; it is enough to make you poor, blind, carnal men, to entertain strange thoughts of me. For, as for my heart, when I go to pray, I find it so loath to go to God, and when it is with him, so loath to stay with him, that many times I am forced in my Prayers, *first* to beg God that he would take mine heart, and set it on himself in Christ, and when it is

---

21 *I will pray with the Spirit*, 246.
22 *I will pray with the Spirit*, 249.
23 *I will pray with the Spirit*, 251.

there, that he would keep it there (Psalm 86.11). Nay, many times I know not what to pray for, I am so blind, nor how to pray, I am so ignorant; only (blessed be Grace) the *Spirit helps our infirmities* [Romans 8:26].

Oh the starting-holes that the heart hath in time of Prayer! none knows how many by-ways the heart hath, and back-lanes, to slip away from the presence of God. How much pride also, if enabled with expressions. How much hypocrisy, if before others. And how little conscience is there made of Prayer between God and the Soul in secret, unless the *Spirit of Supplication* [Zechariah 12:10] be there to help?[24]

This passage displays a couple of the most attractive features of the Puritans: their transparent honesty and in-depth knowledge of the human heart. From personal experience, Bunyan knew well the allergic reaction of the old nature to the presence of God. So, were it not for the Spirit, none would be able to persevere in prayer. Little wonder that Bunyan says right after the above passage (which, it should be noted, concludes with an allusion to Zechariah 12:10): "When the Spirit gets into the heart then there is prayer indeed, and not till then."[25]

Moreover, it is the Spirit who enables a man to know the right and only way to come to God, namely through his beloved Son. "Men may easily say," Bunyan writes, "they come to God in his Son: but it is the hardest thing of a thousand to come to God aright and in his own way, without the Spirit."[26] It is only the Spirit who can enable a person fully conscious of his sinful nature to address God as "Father." Bunyan's discussion of this point is worth quoting in full:

O how great a task is it, for a poor soul that becomes sensible of sin, and the wrath of God, to say in Faith, but this one word, *Father*! I tell you, however hypocrites think, yet the Christian, that is so indeed, finds all the difficulty in this very thing, it cannot say, God is its *Father*.

---

24 *I will pray with the Spirit*, 256–257.
25 *I will pray with the Spirit*, 257.
26 *I will pray with the Spirit*, 251.

Oh! saith he, I dare not call him Father; and hence it is, that the Spirit must be sent into the hearts of God's people for this very thing, to cry, Father, Gal. 4.6, it being too great a work for any man to do *knowingly*, and *believingly*, without it. When I say, *knowingly*, I mean knowing what it is to be a Child of God, and to be born again. And when I say, *believingly*, I mean, for the soul to believe, and that from good experience, that the work of Grace is wrought in him: this is the right calling of God *Father*; and not as many do, say in a babbling way, the Lord's Prayer (so called) by heart, as it lyeth in the words of the Book. No, here is the life of Prayer, when in, or with the Spirit, a man being made sensible of sin, and how to come to the Lord for mercy; he comes, I say, in the strength of the Spirit, and cryeth, *Father*.

That one word spoken in Faith, is better than a thousand prayers, as men call them, written and read, in a formal, cold, lukewarm way.[27]

Here Bunyan speaks from experience. The right calling of God "Father" comes not from the mere recitation of the Lord's prayer "in a babbling way," but from the inner work of the Spirit.[28]

Bunyan refers again to his own experience in prayer when he goes on to stress that only the Spirit can enable the believer to persevere in prayer once he has begun. The Puritans generally emphasized that were it not for the Spirit, none would be able to persevere in prayer. Thus Bunyan could affirm that a "man without the help of the Spirit cannot so much as pray once; much less, continue…in a sweet praying frame."[29]

THE SIGNIFICANCE OF BUNYAN'S TREATISE ON PRAYER

Bunyan's treatise on prayer helped to secure what has become a leading attitude to written and read prayers in evangelical circles: an attitude of extreme wariness. More significantly, Bunyan's treatise can also be seen as a declaration that, without the Spirit, not only our prayer life, but also our entire Christian walk is hollow, stale and life-

---

27 *I will pray with the Spirit*, 252.
28 Greaves, "Introduction," xliii–xliv. See also Nuttall, *Holy Spirit*, 63–65.
29 *I will pray with the Spirit*, 256. See also 256–266.

less. It is often forgotten that Bunyan was a vital participant in what Ronald Reeve has described as the Puritan "rediscovery of the Holy Spirit as the mainspring of all Christian activity."[30] The claim by some contemporary authors and theologians that no post-Reformation movement until this century has really given the Spirit his due is shown to be quite false by the interest that the Puritans had in the person and work of the Spirit.

Bunyan, like most of his fellow Puritans, had an intense desire for the experience of the Spirit, for he knew that the Spirit of Christ alone could lead him to God. Thus, at the conclusion of the treatise, Bunyan expresses the hope that: "Christians...pray for the Spirit, that is, for more of it, though God hath endued them with it already....The Lord in mercy turn the hearts of the people to seek more after the Spirit of Prayer, and in the strength of that, pour out their souls before the Lord."[31]

As John Bunyan lay dying in August 1688, a number of his deathbed sayings were recorded. Among them was one dealing with prayer. "The Spirit of Prayer," he told those gathered to hear his final words, "is more precious than treasure of gold and silver."[32] It was Bunyan's conviction of the work of the Spirit in prayer and preaching which had led him in the first place to embrace an ecclesial position outside of the Church of England. Clearly, as this dying statement shows, it was this conviction that sustained him to the end of his life.[33]

---

30 "John Wesley, Charles Simeon, and the Evangelical Revival," *Canadian Journal of Theology*, 2 (1956): 205.

31 *I will pray with the Spirit*, 271, 285.

32 *Mr. John Bunyan's Dying Sayings* in *The Works of John Bunyan* (John Ball, 1850), I, 47.

33 Richard L. Greaves, "Conscience, Liberty, and the Spirit: Bunyan and Non-conformity" in Keeble, ed., *John Bunyan*, 43.

12

A concluding word

I remember the days of old; I meditate on all that you have done; I ponder the work of your hands.
—PSALM 143:5 (ESV)

The ability to adapt to varied cultural circumstances has been a strength of evangelical Christianity. The downside, though, of this versatility has been the fact that in the past couple of hundred years there has been an ahistorical trajectory at work in the original cultural matrix of evangelicalism, namely, the West. With ever-increasing momentum, Western intellectuals, authors, and educators have been wary of viewing the past as a repository of wisdom. In fact, the latest literary trends, those of postmodernity, have viewed the whole concept of finding a usable past as a ludicrous venture, since the meaning of the past is totally in the eye of the beholder, and hence utterly compromised by subjectivity. Sensitive to cultural trends, evangelicalism now finds herself caught in the same trajectory. This book, though, has sought to sound a different note: the past can be tremendously helpful in knowing how to live.

I have no interest in seeking to find a golden historical era to which we can retreat from the horrors of modernity and, so cocooned, live out our lives. It is in this age, this place "all in a rookery"—to use a gem of Newfoundland English—that we must live. When I was a young boy, fascinated with history, I ardently wished I could live in another time—that of Achilles and those fabled Greek heroes or that of the days of Roman imperial expansion under Trajan, or with the Yorkists during the so-called Wars of the Roses. But those were boyish dreams that the temporal realities of adulthood have blown away. No, it is in this time with all its challenges that I, and you, must live. Yet, we would be fools indeed if we did not seek to learn from those who have gone before, both their words and their lives. In this, I wholeheartedly affirm the wisdom of the ancients, both Christian and pagan, who sought models for their lives in exemplary figures of their past.[1]

For modern evangelicals who truly desire to have their lives ruled by Scripture, the "canon" for all life and thinking, the Reformers and the Puritans are fabulous mentors, for that too was their deepest wish. That they did not wholly realize this wish is an historical given and a reminder that they were not infallible. Nevertheless, as I hope this book has shown, their spiritual experience, their exegesis of Scripture, and their theology is much needed by modern evangelicals as the latter seek to live up to their name and so be faithful to the gospel in "a crooked and twisted generation" (Philippians 2:15).

---

1   See, for example, Marie Noël Keller, *Priscilla and Aquila: Paul's Coworkers in Christ Jesus* (Collegeville: Liturgical Press, 2010), xi–xii, where Keller compares Seneca, Paul and Luke in this regard.

Index

BOOKS, BIBLES, CONFESSIONS, CREEDS

Deo Optimo et Maximo Gloria
To God, best and greatest, be glory

www.joshuapress.com